THE CORNWALLIS MEMORIAL DECADE

The Complete Story of a Decade of Search,
Discovery and Effort by

The 1805 Club
and
The Milford-on-Sea Historical Record Society

Edited by Peter Turner

Milford-on-Sea
Historical
Record Society

EDITORIAL COMMENTS
From Honorary Editor Peter Turner

The unveiling of a plaque commemorating Admiral Cornwallis, in the grounds of St Ann's Church, His Majesty's Naval Base Portsmouth, was achieved after a decade of research, planning, design and organisation.

The purpose in this special publication is twofold: firstly, to record and commemorate all the efforts of contributors and secondly, of equal importance, to evoke happy memories of the events and occasions.

The 1805 Club and the Milford-on-Sea Historical Record Society (MoSHRS) members have contributed to this publication, which largely consists of reproductions of earlier articles, with some notable additions.

Side images are not captioned (I could not know everybody, so named nobody) and they have been randomly reproduced in order to evoke memories of details, events, places and people involved over the decade.

Some images are repeated – there were only a certain number of people involved so no apologies – except to anyone I failed to include, having only been able to use photographs that had been taken.

Some images are blurred – *non est mea culpa*.

For captions and credits to featured images, see page 108.

Generous financial donations enabled this book to be produced,
personally from John Bewley together with funds from both The 1805 Club and MoSHRS.

Thank you to all contributors and to all who took part in the proceedings in any way.

And finally, to produce a book like this can never be done in splendid isolation, so first of all I want to thank my partner, Liz, for critical help and support and for doing more than her share of the cooking, then Stephen Tregidgo for the idea; Barry Jolly for all his contributions and his tremendous help in putting me right; Stephen Howarth, for his usual background assistance; Kathy Brown for sending me far too many pix to find space for; Stuart Wade for teaching me what a printer needs and to all others who have made useful comments.

Special thanks again to Liz, Stephen, Barry and Stephen for the encouragement
that kept me on the job, when it was seeming difficult.

I finish by confessing that any mistakes are down to me –
I failed to find them and I hope you do the same.

Published 2024 by The 1805 Club — © The 1805 Club 2024
ISBN: 978-1-902392-40-0

This is published with the main body text using Cambria 11pt font with Optima font elsewhere.

Printed in Great Britain by Suffolk Digital Ltd. https://suffolkdigital.co.uk

FOREWORD

By Sir Jonathon Band, GCB, DL
President of The 1805 Club

St Ann's Church (formerly known as Dock Chapel) is the spiritual home of the Royal Navy and lies within His Majesty's Naval Base, Portsmouth. As befits its status as the oldest surviving chapel in a navy yard, this building, erected in 1786, has had Historic England Grade II listing since 1972. What this means is that the building and its environs cannot be altered or added to except under special circumstances.

The 1805 Club, together with the Milford-on-Sea Historical Record Society [MoSHRS], have been honoured by exceptional permission to install in the grounds of St Ann's the memorial stone plaque commemorating the life of Admiral the Honourable Sir William Cornwallis, GCB. This is no small thing, and the site, centred in splendid isolation on the south lawn emphasises the importance attached to this admiral, described accurately in this written memento by Professor Andrew Lambert in his excellent article, "The Sheet Anchor of British Strategy".

Elsewhere in this publication you will read of the application to install a plaque in St Paul's Cathedral. The application failed. This seemed a setback at the time, but it turned out to be a fortunate failure: it resulted ultimately in the plaque's final location, meaning that a greater proportion of visitors who see it will appreciate the importance of Cornwallis in Britain's struggle against Napoleon.

You will similarly read about the decade-long effort that both the Club and MoSHRS have put into the search for Cornwallis and the resultant installation of the plaque. The story of this effort is the subject of this document, because such an effort could not be allowed to simply fade from memory. The 1805 Club has a long-standing record of 'punching above its weight' and this is a fine example of what we are able to achieve with such a good crew when we get a fair wind on our quarter.

Long may the Club's achievements continue to be as successful as this one has been.

Yours Aye,

Jonathon Band

CONTENTS

INTRODUCTION BY STEPHEN TREGIDGO

This book follows discussion between Peter Turner and myself in the Summer of 2023, just before the unveiling ceremony of the memorial to Admiral Cornwallis at St Ann's Church in HM Naval Base, Portsmouth. We realised that, almost to the day, the unveiling would mark a decade of work between The 1805 Club and the Milford-on-Sea Historical Record Society to find out more about the Admiral, after prompting by John Bewley (*see page 19*).

We knew that in publications of both The 1805 Club and MoSHRS over the decade there had been numerous articles detailing:

- progress being made in finding out more about the Admiral and his associates;
- the restoration of the ledger marking the grave of the Admiral in All Saints Churchyard, Milford-on-Sea;
- developments and plans for the bi-centenary commemoration events in Milford-on-Sea and the New Forest during the summer of 2019;
- the efforts to get a national memorial to Cornwallis installed at St Ann's Church, HM Naval Base, Portsmouth.

With this decade of work, the moment needed to be marked. We thought a publication detailing how it started, what went on through the decade, and how it concluded, would be most fitting. So this book aims to do all that.

Starting with the Memorial Service and Dedication of the Cornwallis Stone at St Ann's Church, we have the address at the service given by The Reverend James Francis, Chaplain of HMS *Excellent*; and the speech of Professor Andrew Lambert given after the buffet lunch in the grounds of Admiralty House which followed the service and dedication.

Thereafter, generally in chronological order from the start of the 'Cornwallis decade' in May 2013, the book comprises articles recording the progress being made in finding the grave marking the Admiral's resting place at All Saints Church, Milford-on-Sea: the efforts required to restore the ledger; the relationships he had with his Flag Captain, John Whitby and John's wife and their living together in Milford-on-Sea; the plans for the summer-long commemoration in July 2019 of the bi-centenary of the Admiral's death in Milford-on-Sea; and finally the efforts to get a national memorial to Cornwallis installed somewhere that would be fitting to the Admiral's remarkable service to his country.

As you will see, there are numerous pictures covering many of the decade's events, together with random photographs of people who worked on those events or who attended them.

This book becomes a record in its own right of a decade spent by two organisations working in partnership to create a lasting memorial to Admiral Sir William Cornwallis. 🌐

WILLIAM CORNWALLIS:
DEDICATION OF MEMORIAL AT ST ANN'S HM NAVAL BASE
Given by The Reverend James Francis, Chaplain of HMS *Excellent* and Member of The 1805 Club

"...they shall be as mighty men, which tread down their enemies in the mire of the battle."
Zechariah 10:5

One of the best motivational speakers I have heard in recent years was Hon Capt Pete Reed RNR when he visited Britannia Royal Naval College at Dartmouth to speak to the officer cadets about leading to win. A triple Olympic gold medallist, he suffered from a spinal stroke in September 2019 and was paralysed from the chest down. You could hear a pin drop as Pete spoke from his wheelchair about how you train your mind to adopt a winning mindset by setting challenging goals and how you lead a team to win. It became very clear to me that despite the paralysis he remained a *mighty man* to use the Biblical phrase we've just heard Lynda Sebbage read from the prophet Zechariah. Despite his catastrophic injury Pete Reed's good grace and stamina continues to inspire and lead. A *mighty man* indeed!

This sort of stoicism is not a new phenomenon to the Royal Navy. Our most celebrated hero, Horatio Nelson, was wounded yet continued to inspire and lead. Ironically in today's Royal Navy Nelson wouldn't pass a medical employability board! But it is for Nelson's friend, Admiral of the Red, The Hon Sir William Cornwallis, Knight Grand Cross of the Most Honourable Order of the

Bath, that we gather today as we remember Cornwallis, commemorate his inspiring leadership, the enduring debt our nation owes him and unveil a memorial to his immortal memory.

What are the ingredients that make for such a leader, such a *mighty man*, such a person as William Cornwallis?

Is it breeding, education and brain power that simply sets you off to a good start? Is it training and grit, finely honed by commitment, discipline and character? Is it luck topped up with courage – being in the right place at the right time? William Cornwallis had all of these.

He was born in Suffolk in 1744, the fourth son of the 1st Earl Cornwallis. William's family consisted of an impressive line-up of achievers and *mighty men*. There was obviously a religious gene in the family – not uncommon in those days: he had

a brother who became Bishop of Lichfield, an uncle who was Archbishop of Canterbury and his older brother Charles was a General. General Cornwallis was probably the most famous in the family because of his role in the American War of Independence, ending up as Governor General of India.

At the age of 9 William was sent to Eton (or Slough Grammar, as I heard it referred to this week) and after just two years he joined the navy in 1755. After serving in a series of ships he was made Fourth Lieutenant at the grand old age of 17. A year later he promoted to Commander then Post Captain at the age of 21. Many a young naval officer today would give their right arm for such accelerated promotion!

Serving almost everywhere that mattered, he was showered with praise for his courage and honour as a commander and applauded for the discipline of his ship's company. Cornwallis so distinguished himself that on his return to England he was summoned to update the King on affairs in America.

I mentioned that Cornwallis was a friend of Nelson – and whilst in command of HMS *Lion* (a 64-gun third-rate ship of the line) Cornwallis looked after him when they were on passage back

to England after Nelson took ill during the San Juan expedition.

In 1787 Cornwallis was distinguished with the honorary title of *Colonel of Marines* and it wasn't long before he was promoted rear-admiral, and raised his flag at Portsmouth aboard HMS *Excellent*.

Cornwallis made good appointments, attracting the best captains, and was obviously a good judge of character. He had the reputation of being an excellent mentor to his young officers – and set them a great example.

From January 1795 he served as the second-in-command of the Channel Fleet and, as a full admiral in 1801, he took over from Admiral Jervis as the Commander-in-Chief, hoisting his flag at Torbay aboard HMS *Ville de Paris* before making sail to enforce a close blockade of Brest.

Quintin Barry in his book about the blockade of Brest from 1793-1815 writes:

Throughout the long drawn out war at sea during the French Revolutionary and Napoleonic Wars, it was a cardinal principle of British naval strategy to blockade the port of Brest, the largest and most important of the French naval bases that threatened the security of the British Isles. It was a strategy that had been perfected during the Seven Years War, when it culminated in the stunning victory of Quiberon Bay. The American naval historian A.T. Mahan memorably summed up the contribution of the Royal Navy to the ultimate defeat of Napoleon when he wrote: 'Those far distant, storm-beaten ships, upon which the Grand Army never looked, stood between it and the domination of the world.' .... Inevitably, there were great sea battles when the French ventured out, though fewer than might have been expected. For many months at a time the British fleet was at sea off Brest facing the considerable dangers of wind and weather without encountering its adversary.

Cornwallis was key in enabling the victory at Trafalgar, by his command of the Channel Fleet and holding the destiny of the Royal Navy in his hands.

By 1806, in poor health, Cornwallis struck his flag and retired to his estate at Milford-on-Sea. Despite being MP he never spoke in Parliament and rarely attended – so it was said of him that he was a reluctant politician. He clearly preferred to be at sea and visiting remote lands rather than in the midst of society.

A man of few words, it is said that he was modest, warm-hearted, popular for being so 'able and tough' but also a bit eccentric. Nonetheless a *'mighty man.'*

I had the privilege of meeting another *mighty man* of war earlier this week, Lt Col Chris Keble DSO, who served in the Falklands and took command of 2 PARA at a crucial stage during the Battle of Goose Green following the death of the Battalion CO, Lt Col H Jones.

Chris Keeble told me that you needed just three mottos as a wartime leader: be prepared; be ready for anything and do not be afraid.

In the uncertainty of the sea battles of the Georgian Navy I think those same mottos would have stood the test, just as they have since.

So we give thanks today that Admiral William Cornwallis was prepared, ready for anything and was not afraid. We give thanks for his vital role in saving our country from invasion and we give thanks for our Royal Navy today, that (as we stand on the shoulders of giants, *mighty men* such as Admiral Cornwallis) we may continue to be inspired to protect the United Kingdom and its interests around the globe. Amen. ❂

ADMIRAL SIR WILLIAM CORNWALLIS: THE SHEET ANCHOR OF BRITISH STRATEGY

Talk given on 16 June 2023, in the garden of 2SL's Residence, by Professor Andrew Lambert FKC

Although largely forgotten by historians, because he never fought a major battle, Admiral Sir William Cornwallis commanded the main British fleet during the critical years of the Revolutionary and Napoleonic Wars, 1800-05. His appointment as the senior Admiral afloat was entirely appropriate, for he possessed that rare combination of professional skill and enduring temperament required for high command. While he was an old and close friend of Nelson the two men could hardly have been more dissimilar in character. As Mahan observed, Cornwallis

never won a victory, nor had a chance of winning one; but in command both of ships and of divisions, he repeatedly distinguished himself by successfully facing odds which he could not overcome.

These qualities led First Lord of the Admiralty Earl St. Vincent to entrust him with command of the Channel, or Grand, Fleet in 1801 and again in 1803. St. Vincent, who had preceded him, knew that the Western Approaches were the pivot of British strategy, upon which insular security, the defence of trade, economic prosperity and the development of British offensive strategies ultimately depended. While Cornwallis's principal task was to prevent the French from sending their main fleet, based at Brest, into *la*

Manche, to link up with Napoleon's army and invasion shipping at Boulogne, he was also responsible for squadrons blockading Rochefort, L'Orient and Ferrol. The valuable convoys that frequently passed through his station were equally significant. While St.Vincent selected the dynamic, aggressive and impulsive Nelson to command in the Mediterranean, where risks could and, in the event, were run he wanted an altogether different man for the Channel. Cornwallis had built a peerless reputation as a fleet commander and tactician, on the defensive against superior forces. While Nelson might annihilate the enemy Cornwallis would not be defeated, and possessed the temperament and resilience for a monotonous, dreary and yet dangerous task. The selection was inspired.

In 1805, after St. Vincent had left office, Cornwallis and Nelson played out their assigned roles, just as the Earl had anticipated. Cornwallis anchored British strategy, his fleet the central point on which all other fleets could fall back. Because he had pinned the French Admiral Ganteaume's 21 sail of the line inside Brest, Nelson was able to pursue Villeneuve to the West Indies, while other squadrons escorted convoys and supported amphibious offensives in other theatres. In 1805 the Channel Fleet stood between Bonaparte and European hegemony.

The decisions Cornwallis took in August 1805 prevented a French invasion, ensuring that by the time Trafalgar was fought Napoleon was marching on Vienna, and Villeneuve heading to Sicily.

The supreme crisis of the war began with Bonaparte ordering Ganteaume to sea. On 21 August 1805 the entire French fleet left the *Rade* and anchored in Bertheaume Bay. Cornwallis quickly closed in. Unable to attack that evening he conducted a thorough recon-naissance and anchored his seventeen battleships nearby, off the Black Rocks. At 4.30 the following morning Cornwallis, in his flagship, the *Ville de Paris*, weighed and stood toward the enemy leading the fleet in a single line ahead. Initially the French made sail for open water, but as the British closed they went about and scurried backed inside the

Goulet, under the cover of powerful shore batteries. Having secured the strategic object Cornwallis tried to cut off a flagship at the rear of the French line, but Ganteaume scrambled back inside the *Rade*, ending any risk of an invasion. The aggressive side of Cornwallis's his nature, and a well-founded confidence in his people, was tempered by cool judgement, and strategic wisdom. While he would have preferred to let Ganteaume put to sea, where he could be annihilated, Cornwallis knew the strategic situation required the French should be driven back into harbour. Like Nelson Cornwallis's greatness lay in his ability to see the big picture, and adapt his tactics accordingly. Lacking the numbers to be certain of annihilating the enemy he had to be content with a partial action, the moral significance of which was as great as any

fleet battle. The precipitate retreat of the French demonstrated that there was no danger of an invasion. Anticipating the enemy's next move he ordered Admiral Sir Robert Calder to pursue Villeneuve, if he left Ferrol, and advised Collingwood to expect the enemy at Cadiz, decisions that made Trafalgar possible. After Nelson's victory the fleet was divided, to cruise in defence of trade, emphasising the reality that the primary concern throughout the season had been for the defence of trade, not an invasion.

Deeply affected by the death of his friend Nelson, exhausted in mind and body, and convinced there would be no more fleet actions, Cornwallis's mood darkened. The death of Pitt and a change of Government saw him superseded by St. Vincent.

Hauling down his flag on 22 February 1806, the death of his brother in India, followed by that of Flag Captain, John Whitby, on 6 April 1806, marked the end of Cornwallis's earthly ambitions. He retired from public life, living quietly in Hampshire, with his horses and parrots: he had few close friends, and little interest in society at large. At the peace he was awarded the Grand Cross of the Bath. He died on 5 July 1819, and buried in Milford churchyard, alongside Captain Whitby, in an unmarked grave.

Cornwallis preferred the company of other naval men, positively disliked society ashore, considered all forms of outward show vulgar and loathed blood sports. Universally admired and respected by his officers, and loved by the sailors, his nicknames were all complimentary. The lower deck used 'Billy Blue' from constant use of Blue-Peter to keep fleet at short notice while lying in Torbay. His other nick-names, 'Mr Whip' and 'The Coachee', referenced his hard-driving command style. Although prone to depression and ill-humour, he was always cheered by prospect of action.

Professional to the core of his being, William Cornwallis demonstrated the highest qualities of an admiral, his leadership, vision and determination were unsurpassed, and only the accident of history, the one that denied him the great battle he would surely have won, kept him out of the pantheon of naval immortals. It was his lot to endure a career of hard, unrewarding service. Although he never had the opportunity to win a great victory, his pivotal role in the years of maximum danger, between 1800 and 1805, reflected exceptional leadership, judgement and professional qualities of the highest order. Like his friend Nelson he had the insight to function at the highest level, and the steadiness to do it at the one place where the war could be lost. Rather than defeating a French fleet he secured a greater victory, the defeat of Napoleon's strategy. His blockade of the iron-bound coast of Britanny, through all seasons and all weathers will remain for all time the ultimate achievement of sea-power in the age of sail. He should be remembered as the Admiral who held the centre, around which the greatest contest between the land and the sea power was played out. He deserves his place here, and remains an example to all who follow his calling.

Thank you:
Please allow me to propose a toast,
'To the Memory of Admiral Sir William Cornwallis, the greatest of Nelson's contemporaries, the man who held the centre'.

BILLY BLUE

An anonymous popular sea song written in praise of
Admiral the Honourable Sir William Cornwallis during his lifetime.

1

'Tis a terrible time for Englishmen:
All tyrants do abhor them;
Every one of them has to fight with ten,
And the Lord alone is for them.
But the Lord has given the strong right hand,
And the courage to face the thunder;
If a Frenchman treads this English land,
He shall find his grave thereunder.

Britannia is the Ocean-Queen,
and she standeth staunch and true,
With Nelson for her faulchion keen,
and her buckler Billy Blue.

2

They are mustering on yon Gallic coasts,
You can see them from this high land,
The biggest of all the outlandish hosts
That ever devoured an island.
There are steeds that have scoured the Continent,
Ere ever one might say "Whoa, there!"
And ships that would fill the Thames and Trent,
If we would let them go there.

But England is the Ocean-Queen,
and it shall be hard to do;
Not a Frenchman shall skulk in between
herself and her Billy Blue.

3

From the smiling bays of Devonshire
To the frowning cliffs of Filey,
Leaps forth every son of an English sire,
To fight for his native isley.
He hath drawn the sword of his father now
From the rusty sheath it rattled in;
And Dobbin, who dragged the peaceful plough,
Is neighing for the battle-din.

For Albion still is Ocean-Queen,
And though her sons be few,
They challenge the world with a dauntless mien,
And the flag of Billy Blue.

4

Then pledge me your English palm, my lad;
Keep the knuckles for Sir Frenchman;
No slave can you be till you change your dad,
And no son of yours a henchman.
The fight is to come; and we will not brag
Nor expect whatever we sigh for,
But stand at the rock that bears the flag
Our duty is to die for.

For Englishmen confront serene
Whatever them betideth;
And England shall be Ocean's Queen
As long as the world abideth.

A COLLABORATIVE JOURNEY
MILFORD-ON-SEA HISTORICAL RECORD SOCIETY AND THE 1805 CLUB
By Chris Hobby

For MoSHRS this collaborative journey of 10 years' duration with The 1805 Club has brought numerous challenges but also opportunities to grow and develop from a provincial local historical society to a respected charitable society, now known not only within Hampshire but also further afield.

During this journey we have become a Charitable Incorporated Organisation in order to obtain financial assistance in the form of grants from other charitable trusts and in particular from The National Heritage Lottery Fund. Without this status we would have found it impossible to have raised the £50,000 needed to fund all the planned events to commemorate the bi-centenary of the death of Admiral Sir William Cornwallis in 2019

For any successful event, teamwork and close collaboration is essential and the appointment of Stephen Tregidgo as the representative from The 1805 Club proved him to be the ideal person. As a result, both organisations have worked closely together and have "sung from the same hymn sheet". MoSHRS have been able to draw on our members' talents and business expertise in seeking grants. Our "man of words", Barry Jolly, provided many articles on Cornwallis, both for our *Occasional Magazine* and *The*

Kedge Anchor, together with other nautical magazines, raising in the process our Society's profile. Barry's dedication to research has ultimately led to the use of the Admiral's God-daughter's words being used on his commemorative memorial stone at St Ann's Church in the Naval Dockyard at Portsmouth.

Initially, whilst John Bewley of The 1805 Club believed that the admiral lies buried somewhere in All Saints' churchyard it was MoSHRS member Anne Braid who actually discovered the lost John Whitby ledger, beneath which the Admiral is buried. The enthusiasm of the then Chairman of The 1805 Club, the late Peter Warwick, provided the vision and encouragement to us to "aim high". This resulted in James Brown from the New Forest National Park Authority and Rosalyn Goulding from the St Barbe Museum in Lymington (who took over the initial work undertaken by Pam Perry, a trustee of St Barbe's who had originally thought about staging an exhibition), working with the MoSHRS team to stage what turned out to be one of the museum's most successful exhibitions to date. With the successful obtaining of two paintings of national importance from Tate Britain the exhibition entitled "Command of the Seas, The Navy and the New Forest against Napoleon."

With the support of the New Forest National Park Authority, the Honourable Mary Montagu-Scott of Buckler's Hard and The Lymington and District Historical Society, we were able to create the Admirals' Heritage Trail which, like the Admiral's memorial at Portsmouth, is a continuing legacy of Cornwallis and our local admirals of the Georgian period.

So what have we achieved by working together? A three-month exhibition, the creation of the Heritage Trail and a national service of commemoration on the bi-centenary of Cornwallis's death attended by the Lord-Lieutenant of Hampshire, the Earl and Countess Howe and representatives from all levels of government and distinguished naval representatives and personnel from two naval bases and the crew of HMS *Trumpeter.* Following the service at All Saints' Church there was the enactment of Bringing Home the news of Trafalgar and the death of Nelson, organised by Kathy Brown. Local school children received a presentation on the Georgian Navy which provided them the basis to give their interpretation of the Battle of Trafalgar on the village green during the reception following the church service. Here also we witnessed the first rendition of a 1905 composition entitled "Billy Blue" (Cornwallis's nickname) sung by a local choir. Tea and cake was enjoyed by about 350 people courtesy of the Milford Women's Institute members. "A truly quintessential English event "was how Earl Howe described the day.

The main event was followed the next day by a joint visit to Buckler's Hard and boat trip up Beaulieu River. Then in the evening there was a formal dinner at the South Lawn Hotel which rounded off the series of events. And finally, after a delay, due to Covid, came the siting and dedication of the national memorial at St Ann's Church in Portsmouth Dockyard to our Admiral Sir William Cornwallis in June last year.

We can justifiably feel a sense of satisfaction for all that we have achieved together in raising the profile of one of Britain's unsung heroes, whose contribution to our maritime history is now more fully appreciated. ⚓

THE LOCATION SEARCH FOR A NATIONAL REMEMBRANCE STONE HONOURING ADMIRAL SIR WILLIAM CORNWALLIS
By Stephen Tregidgo

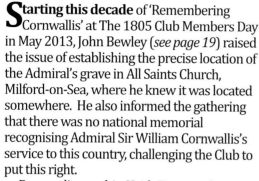

Starting this decade of 'Remembering Cornwallis' at The 1805 Club Members Day in May 2013, John Bewley (*see page 19*) raised the issue of establishing the precise location of the Admiral's grave in All Saints Church, Milford-on-Sea, where he knew it was located somewhere. He also informed the gathering that there was no national memorial recognising Admiral Sir William Cornwallis's service to this country, challenging the Club to put this right.

Responding to this, Keith Evans and Ken Flemming offered to make contact with All Saints Church in Milford-on-Sea. Their record of that contact and first visit is recorded on page 21 obviating the necessity to recount it here as well. Suffice to say, together with the Milford-on-Sea Historical Record Society (MoSHRS), they located the ledger under which the Admiral lay. They also established that other Admirals of this period were also buried in the church and further meetings involving The 1805 Club and MoSHRS led to the restoration and renovation of the ledger.

Efforts at this time were mostly concentrated on conserving and restoring the ledger, involving specialist expertise and ensuring the financing for such (*see article 'An Exciting Joint Project —' on page 35 to 37*). However, The 1805 Club, through John Bewley in 2017 and with the support of MoSHRS, did raise with St Paul's Cathedral authorities an outline proposal and justification for a plaque to Cornwallis to be raised there.

The response at the time was encouraging, but stated that the Cathedral's policy on monuments/memorials/plaques was being reconsidered and, together with Cathedral personnel changes, a formal proposal would be

considered at a later date. It was decided to pursue this later because, not only were The 1805 Club and MoSHRS concentrating on the ledger conservation/restoration, but also deciding to mark the bicentenary of Cornwallis' death in July 2019 with a range of events over that summer in Milford-on-Sea.

In the meantime, MoSHRS took the lead-partner role on the planning, organising and delivering of the summer-long series of events in and around Milford-on-Sea. The 1805 Club was very active in its supporting role, both with direct personal involvement as well as financial and other help such as with The Trafalgar Way post chaise being present on the actual date of the Admiral's death, and work with the local primary school on the 'Wooden Walls Project'. Again this is documented in other pages of this book (*see pages 38 & 48*)

There is of course, the memorial in All Saints Church commissioned by Mrs Theresa West (daughter of Cornwallis's Flag Captain, John Whitby) and John's wife (also called Theresa) which honours Theresa West's mother and father - and also the Admiral (*see mainly page 84*). And as part of the bicentenary commemorations in July 2019, a new memorial window in All Saints' church honouring the three Admirals Cornwallis, Peyton and Man was dedicated by the Rt Rev David Williams, Bishop of Basingstoke. More can be read about this on pages 59 and 60.

Following the very successful 2019 summer of events 'Remembering Cornwallis' in Milford-on-Sea and the wider New Forest, there remained the question of what to do about the lack of a national remembrance plaque/stone honouring Cornwallis.

Subsequent to the initial approach to St

Paul's Cathedral in 2017, Bill White, Chair of The 1805 Club in 2018, at the Club's Trafalgar Night Dinner that year, sat at the same table as the Club's Guest of Honour, The Rt Honourable Earl Howe. Bill took the opportunity to raise with Earl Howe the possibility of the Earl proposing to the St Paul's Cathedral authorities for the placement of a plaque to Admiral Sir William Cornwallis in the crypt of the Cathedral near Lord Nelson's tomb.

Bill duly followed up that early approach explaining why it was felt that St Paul's would be an appropriate place for a plaque, given that the Admiral was not only a close friend of Lord Nelson, but also because, in the south transept of the cathedral, there is a statue of the Admiral's elder brother, General Charles Cornwallis, 1st Marquess Cornwallis. Charles Cornwallis was the General who surrendered the British Army at Yorktown to a combined American and French army thereby losing the American 'colonies'. His career, although redeemed in part by service in India, could be said to be less distinguished than his younger, naval brother.

To reinforce the above approach, Bill had also managed to elicit support for an approach to be made to the Cathedral authorities from leading naval historians Professor Andrew Lambert and Dr Nicholas Rodger. Further, Bill knew that The 1805 Club president, Admiral Sir Jonathon Band would be in support and believed the then First Sea Lord, Admiral Sir Philip Jones and Admiral of the Fleet Lord Boyce would be like-minded.

In discussion with the Preceptor of the Cathedral at the Wreath Laying Ceremony at Nelson's Tomb in that year's (2018) Trafalgar Day event, Bill understood that Cathedral policy on new monuments was very strict and gaining institutional support for such would be very desirable. Bill felt that given The 1805 Club's excellent links with both the National Maritime Museum and the National Museum of the Royal Navy, support for a Memorial proposal to the Cathedral would be forthcoming from these institutions.

With all this support for the concept, Earl Howe wrote to the cathedral authorities seeking consent for the erection of a plaque. It was very surprising, not to say very disappointing, when a refusal was received from the Dean.

Thoughts then turned to what other location would be appropriate for a memorial to Admiral Cornwallis, and this led to an approach being made to Portsmouth Cathedral. But, somewhat surprisingly, this too met with a refusal, but triggered another suggestion in Portsmouth.

As Sir Jonathon said in his Foreword, St Ann's Church in His Majesty's Naval Base Portsmouth is the spiritual home of the Royal Navy. What is more, the present church, having been built in 1786, would have been where Admiral Sir William Cornwallis, when in Portsmouth, would have worshipped. Being a Portsmouth MP as well as Commander-in-Chief of the Channel Fleet, he would have known the Church well.

An approach was made to St Ann's church authorities. It resulted in a visit to the church by Bill and Sheila White, Admiral Sir Jonathan Band, Chris Hobby of MoSHRS and Stephen Tregidgo in September 2020. Discussion took place with the Rev Adam Gay, the then Chaplain, about how best to make a formal proposal and to see where within the church might be an appropriate site for a plaque. It ended with the conclusion that St Ann's would be a very appropriate place, with the next step being to make a formal application to the Chaplaincy Council of St Ann's Church.

Our preferred location in the chancel was unacceptable because a Listed Building Regulation stipulated that no further plaques/memorials were to be erected there. Another visit was organised in December 2020 to identify a suitable location outside the chancel. This was then submitted to the Chaplaincy Council, together with information on the size and wording to be used on the brass plaque.

We were asked to submit another proposal for a smaller plaque to be located in a different, less contentious part of the church. Both MoSHRS and The 1805 Club felt that the concept of a national memorial to a distinguished Admiral in a prestigious location had now been devalued to such an extent that it no longer did service to the Admiral or warranted the expense to both organisations in obtaining a plaque and arranging for its placement. At that point the application was paused.

In the late summer of 2021 the application was then resubmitted, leading to a very much more positive response agreeing to a grander, larger plaque than that previously proposed, to be submitted with a suitable inscription incised on stone and to be erected high on the north wall of the church near the pulpit. The 1805 Club and MoSHRS were delighted.

Stephen Tregidgo approached a number of memorial stonemasons local to Portsmouth and commissioned South Coast Memorials in Fareham to do the work. Work was then done on producing the wording for the memorial stone and, of course, its layout and design. A number of drafts and designs were considered, all of which involved South Coast Memorials.

Finally, the wording and design as shown in the frontispiece was approved by the Council of The 1805 Club and the Trustees of MoSHRS – both organisations sharing the substantial cost of this magnificent memorial. South Coast Memorials were very professional throughout the commission and delivered an exemplary result as shown by any photographs of the memorial in situ in this book.

We began to think that after all this time, we were going to meet the challenge that John Bewley had set back in May 2013. However, there was to be one further, unexpected, major setback to overcome before the project could be realised. It was nearly terminal too, but as often happens, when one door closes another, often

better one, opens. And it was so with this 'hiccup'.

An October 2022 site meeting with South Coast Memorials to scope out how to fix the memorial to the church wall was arranged. With the marble stone commissioned and part paid for, with the Cornwallis Coat of Arms and the logos of The 1805 Club and MoSHRS beautifully carved into the marble awaiting the words to be carved and painted in, South Coast Memorials declared that to mount the marble on the church wall identified would be, technically, a near impossibility. They explained that with the weight of the marble and the state of the church wall the cost of securing it there would be almost prohibitive.

Chris Hobby, the Rev Phill Amey (who had now succeeded Adam Gay) and I gulped, gulped some more, and then some more — and then we started to look all around the church again for an alternative location. We eventually hit on the idea of locating it outside the church where there were two small square lawns within the consecrated ground of the church. Hit by a second world war bomb, the area marked where the church had originally extended to but had not been rebuilt over.

We all thought the new location was so much better than the original. Here it would be at ground level – not high on a wall, and here it would be viewed by everyone going in and out of the church – not just those sitting by the pulpit. In short, it was a most fitting, prominent, location where it could be seen and read very easily by everyone.

South Coast Memorials then went ahead to put in place the foundations to support it, the 'wedge' to angle it and finally the marble stone upon the whole. All was now in place to end the Cornwallis Remembered Decade with the June 2023 St Ann's Church Commemoration Service and the formal unveiling of the Cornwallis National Memorial by Nigel Atkinson Esq, HM Lord-Lieutenant of Hampshire. 🏵

THE REASON WHY

By John Bewley MBE TD MA.

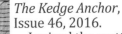

With a keen interest in the Naval history of the Napoleonic wars, in 2011–12 I was researching the defence of Britain in the early 1800s.

It became clear that Admiral Cornwallis had been a key player but I could find little about his personal life. Further research yielded fascinating details.

Starting with Professor Lambert's Dictionary of National Biography entry, attributing the Admiral's blockade of Brest as "the ultimate achievement of sea power in the age of sail", several days in the archives of the National Maritime Museum seemed justified.

Sorting through boxes of the then un-catalogued papers of Cornwallis, his will and other documents put flesh on the bones and provided a wealth of detail, including significant bequests to ladies of his acquaintance during his West Indies posting.

However, I could find no evidence of a memorial to this remarkable man, other than a factually incorrect plaque in the Royal Garrison Church, Portsmouth, and his grave at Milford-on-Sea. Full details of this, together with the magnificent Communion silver commissioned in his memory by Theresa Cornwallis-West, were published in

The Kedge Anchor, Issue 46, 2016.

I raised the matter at the 2014 AGM of the Club. Ken Flemming and Keith Evans promptly visited Milford and thus began the warm relationship with MoSHRS.

With the support of Bill White and Peter Warwick, and supported by the then Chaplain to the Fleet, I prepared a paper with a view to a plaque in St. Paul's Cathedral. This, with a similar attempt at Portsmouth, failed.

During this period, I had a lengthy exchange of emails with Alan Schom, who, in "Trafalgar, Countdown to Battle" regarded the failure to honour Cornwallis as "a distortion of modern British history".

In 2019, through a well-placed Royal Navy friend, the late HRH Prince Philip, Lord High Admiral, expressed his delight that Cornwallis was finally receiving recognition through the bi-centennial event at Milford.

The 1805 Club and MoSHRS pursued the project to a brilliant climax in Portsmouth in June.

In conclusion, all the research indicates that without Cornwallis, there would have been no Trafalgar. ⚓

Editor's Note: Referring to John's final sentence above, it could also be said that without John Bewley there may not have been the Cornwallis memorial that was unveiled in June 2023. Or this book! When Stephen Tregidgo and John Bewley suggested to me keenly that it would be good if we could produce a book recording all the events of the last ten years resulting in this event I offered to tackle it, but the format had to be something worthwhile and the cost would not be trivial. Estimates of cost were obtained and The 1805 Club 'ummed and ahhed', and discussed it with MoSHRS. Then John Bewley contributed generously, and it all immediately became doable. Thank you John.

A POETIC TRIBUTE
By Barry Jolly

Barry Jolly is Editor of *Milford-on-Sea Historical Record Society 'Occasional Magazine'*, with previous articles on Cornwallis published in that journal, *The Trafalgar Chronicle* and *Hampshire Studies*.

During the summer of 2018, and after reviewing the poetry of Mrs Theresa West (*qv*), I found myself pondering the idea of writing a tribute to the admirals of Milford in verse form. Not that I had ever attempted anything so rash previously, but, after mulling over some ideas for a few days, I sat down one rainy Sunday morning to put the idea into effect. Just forty minutes later, the poem, in sonnet form, was complete. There remained some rough edges, it is true, and these took a number of weeks to resolve, but the bulk of the work was done.

Shakespearean scholars may scoff at the rhyming scheme, because it is not in the form popularised by England's greatest playwright. I console myself however, with the thought that the format is known, especially in Australia, as the Bowlesian format, adopted by Revd William Lisle Bowles when his first sonnets were published in 1789. It is contemporary, therefore with the lives of the admirals depicted here.

The Elegy was first published in the Cornwallis Bicentenary Edition of the MoSHRS *Occasional Magazine* in 2019, and subsequently in *The Glazier* (No 58, Summer 2019) in a report on the Three Admirals Window in All Saints Church, Milford. The window itself incorporates the last two lines from the Elegy. ⚓

ELEGY FOR THE ADMIRALS OF MILFORD

On Heart of Oak, brave Jolly Tars their men,[1]
Stand Nelson, Jervis, Howe in *Victory*,[2]
Their names for ever cast in history,
With coronets and ermine granted then.[3]

But what of those who fought the French cockade[4]
'Gainst storm and tide in restless seas that foam
Now buried in remote south Hampshire loam,
Old Boney's plans set nought by close blockade?[5]

Cornwallis, long renown'd for his Retreat,[6]
And Robert Man, good Man in every sense,[7]
John Peyton too, so staunch in his *Defence*;[8]
Three English seamen true: each one to cleat.

With fame and honour and respect well blest,
'Midst Milford's lichen'd graves they now may rest.

From Wikipedia:

Theresa Cornwallis West (née **Whitby**; 1806–1886) (Mrs F. West) was a British author. She is most noted for her A Summer Visit to Ireland in 1846 and wrote stories for children, young adults and even a novel for adults (The Doom of Doolandour). Her travelogue, written as a member of the English upper class visiting Ireland as a tourist, in the early stages of the Famine has proven a valuable source of both information and views. She was born at Newlands Manor, Hampshire to the Royal Navy Captain John Whitby (flag captain for Admiral Sir William Cornwallis) and Mary Anne Theresa Whitby (1783–1850) (née Symonds, the writer, landowner, artist and reintroducer of sericulture to England). Theresa married, in 1827, Frederick Richard West (1799–1862) of Ruthin Castle and unlike his first wife bore children and went on to outlive him.

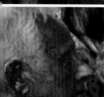

References:

[1] The chorus to William Boyce's *Heart of Oak* – the official march of the Royal Marines – runs:
Heart of Oak are our ships,
Jolly Tars are our men.

[2] Three admirals of the wars against Revolutionary France who achieved at least one major victory at sea. Each at one time or another raised his flag in *Victory*.

[3] Howe and Jervis were both ennobled as earls (hence the coronets and ermine) and Nelson as viscount. Rather bizarrely, Nelson's brother William was advanced to earl in 1805 after Trafalgar.

[4] Widely worn in the early days of the French Revolution.

[5] The Blockade of Brest was the crowning achievement of Cornwallis' career, preventing Napoleon Bonaparte's planned invasion of England.

[6] In 1795, Cornwallis extricated his small force of five ships of the line, two frigates and a brig from an encounter with a French fleet of thirty ships, including no fewer than twelve ships of the line, with considerable skill, thereby establishing his reputation

[7] Nelson, who served under Man in the Mediterranean, described him as 'a good man in every sense of the word'.

[8] Peyton was Captain of the 74 gun *Defence* at the Battle of the Nile in 1798, taking the surrender of the French 80 gun *Franklin*.

THE FIRST REPORT [IN *KA*]
By Kenneth Flemming FM LM, Club Vice President

The first report to appear in The Kedge Anchor *was edition number 39 – Spring 2014 – pages 29-31, reproduced here in full.*

During last year's **Members Day** meeting at the East India Club, one of our members stated with some concern that he believed Admiral Cornwallis was buried in an unmarked grave in Milford churchyard and asked if the Club could look into it. Vice President Keith Evans contacted the church and asked, if indeed, Cornwallis was there and was he in an unrecorded grave. The church authority fortunately passed the question to The Milford-on-Sea Historical Record Society starting a series of events which led to an unusual and absorbing story. It was confirmed in a (now) unrecorded grave Admiral Sir William Cornwallis 1744–1819 lies with his flag Captain John Whitby 1775–1806 together with his wife Mary Ann Theresa Whitby 1784–1850 at All Saints Church. He had been placed in a vault at the west end of the church, but, because of alterations to the church and grave- yard the exact location of the vault is uncertain. Cornwallis had left instructions that no memorial or monument should be

raised to him. However within the church there is a fine marble memorial to the Admiral erected by John Whitby's daughter, Theresa John Cornwallis Whitby.

At the invitation of The Milford-on-Sea Historical Record Society, Keith Evans and myself were asked if we would like to visit All Saints to review the graves and memorials. The visit was to be accompanied by the Vice-Chairman and other research members of the Society. This was arranged and after the introductions

we were shown around the church while being informed of its history and given much detailed information on its naval people interred there.

It was a delight that we were then taken to visit Newlands Manor, the former home of Admiral Cornwallis and his flag Captain John Whitby. Newlands is privately owned and it was a privilege to see the house together with its extensive grounds and lake which are not open to the public.

While it is the graves and memorials that

the Club safeguard, history sometimes records little of the personalities contained within, only their actions. Here at All Saints we have a glimpse of two individuals that are largely unknown in recorded history. However thanks to The Milford-on-Sea Historical Record Society, a very knowledgeable group of people, we can now record something of Captain John Whitby RN and his young wife Mary Ann Theresa Whitby. The story of this quite remarkable woman and her compelling relationship with Admiral Cornwallis will feature in a future issue.

This Hampshire church has its origins around the time of the Domesday Book of 1086 and is of particular interest to the naval historian. Within the church and burial ground lie the remains of several notable naval officers.

Admiral Robert Man 1748–1813 was born into a naval family, his father, the elder Robert Man, was a captain in the navy. He was mortally wounded while commanding HMS Milford during the capture of the French privateer Gloire on 7 March 1762, during the Seven Years War. The younger Robert Man embarked on a naval career and was commissioned as a lieutenant on 26 May 1768 later holding five independent commands.

He was given command of a detached squadron in 1796 and sailed to Gibraltar with seven ships to watch the French fleet at anchor at Cadiz under Admiral Joseph de Richery. His squadron carried supplies for Admiral Sir John Jervis's blockading fleet off Toulon. While returning to Gibraltar Man's squadron, accompanied by three transports and a brig, were sighted

by the Spanish fleet under Don Juan de Lángara, helped by an easterly breeze the Spanish bore up and captured the merchant brig and one of the transports, but Man and his seven ships of the line managed to escape into Rosia Bay, near the mole of Gibraltar. Man held a conference with his

may explain how he reached captain's rank within the service and on retirement through seniority to Rear-Admiral of the Red.

He suffered from ill health and was anxious to go home, but at the Nile he commanded his ship with good sense and courage. Defence had one of the longest sick lists with intermittent fevers accompanied by sore throats and inflammatory complaints. Many of her sailors had scurvy and suffered with persistent sea ulcers caused by unhygienic living conditions and constant exposure to sea water. Defence, the oldest ship at the

captains and decided not to return to the Mediterranean, but instead to sail north with a convoy, and then cruise off Cape Finisterre for a time. With his ships in poor condition after a long period at sea, he then returned to England to refit. Man had no authority to make this decision, and it infuriated Jervis, who accused him of jeopardising the British strategy and forcing a temporary withdrawal from the Mediterranean. Man was ordered to strike his flag and never again received an active command.

Admiral John Goodwin Gregory Peyton 1753–1809 one of the Band of Brothers who commanded HMS Defence at the Battle of the Nile has a memorial here in the centre ailse of the nave. There is also a memorial plaque to him erected by his widow on the wall of the south transept partly obscured by the organ casework. The plaque is in need of some restoration and is difficult to read. John Peyton was the grandson of an admiral, and the son of John (Edward) Joseph Peyton 1725–1806, an elder brother was Rear Admiral Joseph Peyton 1750–1816, while a younger brother was Captain Thomas Peyton RN. John Peyton is described by Andrew Lambert as a man of modest abilities this

Nile was launched in 1763 and had been present in actions under Rodney in India and at the First of June. She was at the time of Peyton's command worn out.

He wrote to Nelson: The rapid decline of my health and bodily strength is such to place me in the most uncomfortable situation in looking to the long continuance of the hot weather that must take place. I feel but to strongly its operation on my constitution will make it very unjustifiable in retaining a situation I shall not be equal to he asked to leave the ship as soon as it was in a suitable port.

Nelson refused his request and as a consequence he fought at the Nile and was one of the more active captains. Engaging at 7pm in a slow and terrible duel with Le Peuple Souerain which lasted three hours before his opponent was totally dismasted and overcome. Defence lost her fore-topmast over the side at the end of the action, just five minutes later he veered away on his sheet anchor in order to get alongside Le Franklin.

Oliver Warner says of this action: Not a moment was lost; not a break for recovery. It is no wonder that the Band of Brothers were invincible.

John Peyton married Susanna Gurnall by licence at St Marylebone, Middlesex on 4 April 1793 and soon after moved to their home Priestlands near Lymington, Hampshire.

There are many other naval connections with the church, including a fine memorial window to Vice Admiral Richard Peacocke who died in 1846.

In the chancel is an elaborate marble memorial to Sir James Rivett-Carnac who in 1836–37 was Chairman of the East India Company and as such was much involved in naval affairs of the time. Another person of interest buried in the churchyard is the pilot of the Titanic who was thought to have been lost but he had left the ship at Cherbourg.

TWO REMARKABLE PEOPLE REDISCOVERED
Captain John Whitby RN
and his redoubtable wife Mary Anne Theresa
Kenneth Flemming

In the Summer of 2014 this article appeared in The Kedge Anchor, *Issue 40, starting on the front cover:*

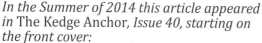

It **is fascinating** when people who in their own lifetimes were quite well known fade from history then reappear in later years. Such is the case with Captain John Whitby RN and his wife Mary Ann Theresa. It is largely due to the efforts of an impressive group of people, the Milford-on-Sea Historical Record Society, that we can return them to their place in history, and add something to that history.

Captain Whitby was the eldest surviving son of the Rev Thomas Whitby of Creswell Hall, Stafford. He was born on 7 October 1774 and entered the service as an AB on 18 April 1787 at the age of 12. In October 1788, ten days after his fourteenth birthday, he joined HMS *Crown* (64), the flagship of the East Indian Squadron under Commodore the Hon. William Cornwallis, as a midshipman. This was the start of flourishing relation- ship with Cornwallis, who was then 44 years old. The passage to India took seven months with both staying in the East for the next four years. Whitby must have impressed with his abilities, because Cornwallis's relationship with him took on a quasi-paternal role. In November

1791, at the age of seventeen years and one month, Whitby passed his Lieutenant's exam on his own ability, proving he could sail a ship and navigate by Mercator projection. His promotion to Master and Commander came on 28 December 1792, commanding HM Sloop *Despatch* (18) on station.

Nelson himself had written to his 'Dear Friend' Cornwallis asking for a placement but Cornwallis knew he had only recently married and for this reason had not suggested his name to the Admiralty. He did later offer a place 'if more ships came out'.

Cornwallis progressed John Whitby quickly, recognising his abilities and character, including a background that was

far from that of the clergy. His father the Rev. Thomas came from a long established Staffordshire family, holding office as a High Sheriff of the county in 1733, and John's grandfather (also Thomas) held the post in 1718. John Whitby's brother Henry also became a captain in the Royal Navy and died at a similar age. John Jervis, Earl St Vincent, a relation of the Whitby family, may also have had some influence over his early career.

Cornwallis was promoted to Rear Admiral in March 1793 whilst flying his flag in HMS *Minerva* (38). Her captain conveniently took passage home, enabling John Whitby to become Flag Captain – the youngest captain in the Navy. He reached

Post rank at the age of eighteen and a half on 20 April 1793.

Lacking some maturity as captain of the *Minerva*, he decided to punish any crew member who swore or used 'profane oaths or cursings' on board with seven lashes of the cat; which not only highlights his family's religious background but more, his youth and inexperience. It displeased the crew very much and provoked a demonstration for this new and singular offence that had suddenly been thrust on them. Whitby with good common sense withdrew the order at the insistence of Cornwallis.

In 1803 Whitby was captain of HMS *Belleisle* (74) in the Mediterranean. Nelson thought highly of him, writing to Cornwallis, 'I have with me an élève of yours whom I esteem most highly, not only as an active officer, but as a gentleman; his ship is always perfectly ready for any service, and he executes in the best style, and I am sure Captain Whitby will give me support in the true Cornwallis style should the French come out'.

There is a very illuminating letter worth quoting in full which highlights the respect and trust that this young captain held while commanding Belleisle.

TO CAPTAIN JOHN WHITBY, H.M. SHIP *BELLEISLE*

Victory, Madalena Island, 3rd January, 1804.

Sir,

I have received your letter of yesterday's date, acquainting me that Thomas Carrol, Quarter-Gunner, belonging to his Majesty's Ship *Belleisle*, under your command, had given himself as a deserter from the Peterel Sloop, having entered for that Vessel previous

LYMINGTON.

Particulars

FREEHOLD PROPERTY,

PRIESTLANDS,

MOST COMFORTABLE RESIDENCE,

Pleasure-Grounds, Gardens, and Plantations,

BOROUGH OF LYMINGTON,
HANTS.

to her being paid off; in answer to which I am to desire you will, whenever the *Belleisle* meets the *Peterel*, if he entered on board her since her being paid off, deliver him up: and you will warn the said Thomas Carrol of the punishment which he merits, and that it is only by his extraordinary good conduct in the *Belleisle* from this time, that [he] can lessen the punishment which a Court-martial may inflict; and that if ever he deserts again, he can expect nothing less than to suffer death. I am, &c. NELSON AND BRONTE.

Thomas Carrol must have had a huge amount of faith and confidence in his captain to give himself up despite the account of his (extra-ordinary) good conduct while serving in *Belleisle*. Whitby must have spoken well of him when informing Nelson and may have delivered some justification for his desertion from *Peterel*.

A further glimpse of his character can be seen when he took the news of Lord Nelson's death to Lady Hamilton on 6 November 1805. Lapenotiere had arrived with Collingwood's dispatches at the Admiralty at 1 a.m. that morning. Whitby was sent by the Admiralty to break the news, but why was a junior captain given the task and why was he at the Admiralty on this particular day?

In his biography *The Pursuit of Victory* (page 528),* Roger Knight writes that on hearing the news at the Admiralty, 'Lord Barham wrote immediately to Fanny, but his Evangelical rectitude prevented a letter to Emma, so he deputed the comptroller of the navy, Sir Andrew Snape Hamond, to write to her'. Lord Barham and Admiral Sir William Cornwallis were in correspondence at the time about the future disposition of the Channel fleet. Cornwallis, naturally accompanied by Whitby, must have been at the Admiralty, both having taken leave from the demands of the service.

Both respected Nelson and that respect was shared. Understanding the relationship with Lady Hamilton Whitby was a natural choice. Admiral Cornwallis would have directed him to deliver the official Admiralty letter before the news was broadcast. Lady Hamilton later recalled to Lady Elizabeth Foster how she had heard the news, "Captain Whitby was unable to speak – tears in his eyes and a deathly paleness over his face made me comprehend him".

In 1800 Cornwallis leased Newlands Manor, Milford, for a period of five years from Sir Hadley d'Oyly for £1,050. It was then a thatched farm-house with sixty-two acres of land. The house was considerably enlarged within the first year.

Captain John Whitby RN married Mary Ann Theresa Symonds at St George's Church, East Stonehouse, Plymouth on 13 October 1802. The couple came to live at Newlands with the Admiral.

On Christmas Day 1802, while the Admiral and John Whitby were away, the house caught fire due to the careless- ness of a servant. The flames being seen by the worshippers in Milford church, all left to help fight the blaze leaving the rather comical figure of the vicar preaching to a disappearing congregation. The Admiral bought the freehold and gave the responsibility of rebuilding Newlands and generally managing the estate to nineteen-year-old Theresa Whitby. She came to live there alone apart from one or two servants while the house swarmed with workmen, supervising the construction and laying out the grounds with trees. During 1804 after a previous miscarriage their daughter Theresa John Cornwallis was born. The Admiral became her godfather and later adopted her.

During 1805 the rebuilding was completed in the present Strawberry Hill Gothic Style. It included twenty-seven bedrooms; in the area of the South Lawn is a school run by the 'Ladies Society for the Education and Employment of the Female Poor'.

Captain John Whitby RN died on 7 April 1806 at Newlands in the prime of life aged thirty. His widow was just twenty-two while their daughter was twelve months old. It was reported in the Naval Chronicle that his death came after a 'rapid and overwhelming progress,' but this may not be the case. It is likely his illness was caused by sea service including long absences away under difficult circumstances which had directly influenced his physical and rational health over many previous months. After writing a very short will on 4 April he became delirious and died three days later. Had he lived four years longer, then, at the age of thirty-five, in accordance with the system of automatic promotion prevailing at the time, he would have achieved flag rank as a Rear Admiral.

In retirement Admiral Cornwallis frequently held large dinner-parties at Newlands but, ever the seaman, he always rose at four a.m. and rode out on his favourite pony from six to eight in all weathers and seasons. Breakfast usually consisted of one half cup of strong green tea without milk or sugar, a thick piece of bread which he toasted himself and ate without butter. A plain lunch followed at one and dinner at six accompanied by a bottle of Port and strong coffee. He loved wildlife which appeared quite tame to him. He disliked fox-hunting and coursing where the animal died by slow torture. The Whitbys' daughter, Theresa John Cornwallis Whitby, illustrates the Admiral's dislike of unmerited honours by recalling an episode when she was very young. When asked by the Admiral what she was doing while reading a book about the peerage, she was told to 'put that nonsense away, half the men in that book are living on the reflected glory of their forebears. Honours are very

well in their way, but remember, "Worth makes the man and want of it the fellow".' Admiral Cornwallis had shunned glory and self-promotion all his life. In his will he left the interest on his entire fortune of £30,000 pounds then eventually the £30,000 itself (with the exception of some small legacies) to Mary Ann Theresa Whitby, in trust for her daughter and her daughter's son, William Cornwallis-West, who was born in 1835 and who eventually received £10,000 pounds. A small additional bequest went to William Symonds, Mary's brother, who used it to launch a successful career in naval architecture.

There was an inordinate bond between Admiral Sir William Cornwallis and the Whitbys that reached back to HMS *Crown*. Shortly before leaving India to return on a passage that would take six months he made a will leaving his possessions to nineteen-year-old John Whitby and his wearing apparel to his servant, Joseph Parsons. In a memo dated 'Minerva at sea, October 1793' he directs: 'I desire that my Body if I die at sea may be sewed up in an old cot or canvass, and thrown from the gangway into the sea in the same manner as the seaman are buried'.

In the same manner he later gave directions as to his funeral, that he was to be 'buried alongside his friend Captain John Whitby in Milford Churchyard'. There was to be no tomb-stone or any kind of memorial to his memory. Mary Ann Theresa Whitby obeyed this last injunction to the letter.

Apart from a short period after Cornwallis's death in July 1819 she continued to live on the estate for the rest of her life, enlarging it in 1829 with the purchase of Milford House and the Manor of Milford Baddesley. An extremely talented and well educated woman, she is described by her daughter on her memorial as 'The affectionate and faithful wife of John Whitby Esq Post Captain Royal Navy',

about silkworms, conducting breeding experiments to help develop his theories of selection. She was also an accomplished artist.

Their daughter Theresa John Cornwallis West (1804– 1886) had inherited £10,000 along with her son and felt such a debt of gratitude to Cornwallis that she overrode his wish that there should be no memorial. Knowing the Admiral well, he has described her as 'a most lovely child'. He died while holding her hand as a thirteen-year-old girl. She not only built a family vault and transferred the coffins of her parents and the Admiral to it but also put up a large memorial tablet in the church itself, pleasing in design and setting out in the best Victorian style the family history, qualities, and achievements of Admiral Sir William Cornwallis G.C.B.

Her motives for doing so are quite clear: in the memorial are inscribed the words 'her daughter Mrs Frederick West feels it her duty to erect to the benefactor who cherished her infancy with parental solicitude, and whose memory she reveres with affection, gratitude, and admiration'.

It remains today in All Saints, Milford-on-Sea, as the only memorial to this great sailor and Englishman.

The recently rediscovered grave of Admiral Sir William Cornwallis G.C.B, John Whitby RN, and Mary Ann Theresa Whitby.

The door is the entrance to the vestry behind which is Admiral Man's gravestone removed from the churchyard and placed there in 1934. The sloping roof to the right is on the north side of the church tower.

It is due to the efforts of Bob Braid and the MoSHRS that the gravesite has been formally identified.

So fundamental to this story, the portraits were painted at differing times and in different styles. There is much detail in Captain John Whitby's uniform. This would have been painted to show his coming of age and increasing seniority, probably some time

possessing 'unfeigned piety, and masculine sense, with every feminine charm of person, the desire of being useful to her species'. 'Her intellect was penetrating, her accomplishments varied, she was the benefactress of the poor, and the stay of many'.

During 1835 she travelled to Italy where she encountered stories of an English businessman who had made substantial profits from silk-worms on a mulberry plantation near Milan. She hoped to reintroduce sericulture to England not only to make a profit but also to provide employment for poor women. It took ten years until she was able to produce silk economically; the major problem proved to be processing the raw silk, rather than rearing the silk- worms. In 1846 she read a paper on the breeding of silk-worms at a meeting of the British Association for the Advancement of Science in Southampton. Here she met Charles Darwin with whom she corresponded extensively

in 1796. Mary Ann Theresa's portrait shows a young woman reaching the same maturity set against a rich background and with predictable style indicating a gloved hand. It was painted in 1805 following her coming of age in December 1804, eight or nine years after the portrait of Captain Whitby.

The portraits that had once hung at Newlands became the property of a great-grandson of the Whitbys, Major George Frederick Myddelton Cornwallis-West (1874–1951). Shortly before his death he decided to pass them to a family member who could be

relied on to look after them rather than becoming lost in a museum or art gallery's basement. They were passed to Henry Hornyold-Strickland of Sizergh Castle, Kendal, until the castle and the family's collection of portraits were given to the National Trust in 1950. The Hornyold-Stricklands continue to live at Sizergh as tenants and the small group of family portraits from Cornwallis-West remain in their possession and on show to the public.

TWO IMPORTANT MoSHRS PUBLICATIONS:
MoSHRS OCCASIONAL MAGAZINE FOR 2019

The 'Cornwallis bi-centenary edition' of the MoSHRS Occasional Magazine contains articles on Cornwallis together with reasoned - and very positive - assessments of the lives and careers of Admiral Robert Man and Rear Admiral John Peyton. All articles are now available on the MoSHRS website: https://www.milfordhistory.org.uk/

Milford-on-Sea
Historical Record Society

OCCASIONAL MAGAZINE

New Series, Volume 6: Cornwallis bi-centenary edition 2019

MILFORD-ON-SEA HISTORICAL RECORD SOCIETY

Occasional Magazine
New Series, Volume 6 2019

CONTENTS

Editor: Barry Jolly
Published by Milford-On-Sea Historical Record Society
Registered Charity No 1177587
Printed by Smith and Son Printers 74 Station Rd, New Milton BH25 6LE
© Milford-On-Sea Historical Record Society and the Authors
ISSN 1479-4101

AND THE ANOTHER MoSHRS PUBLICATION: MRS WHITBY'S LOCKET

A **Publication** of Milford-on-Sea Historical Record Society by Barry Jolly: Mrs. Whitby's Locket tells the story of a naval officer of some two hundred years ago, John Whitby. He is little known, but deserves better. He was promoted to Post Captain at a younger age than Nelson, and received his first command whilst still a Midshipman at the age of sixteen years and two months. His rapid advancement was aided in no small measure by an interconnecting web of contacts and men of influence, not least of whom was Admiral Sir William Cornwallis.

Mrs. Whitby married at a young age, and within just a few months found herself in charge of the rebuilding of Cornwallis' house, Newlands at Milford, Hampshire, and running, and developing, his estate. When he died, he left his entire fortune to her and her daughter

The permanent link between Captain and Mrs Whitby was Admiral Cornwallis. All three had a hand in the production of an enamelled locket which symbolises the enduring nature of their loyalty and devotion during the wars against the French and which gives this story its name. The locket, having been sold by their great grandson in 1923, now resides in the Victoria and Albert Museum. 🌀

For a complete list of relevant publications by MoSHRS go to page 110 (inside back cover)

AN EXCITING JOINT PROJECT OF CONSERVATION AND RESTORATION OF THREE NATIONALLY IMPORTANT NAVAL MEMORIALS

By Kenneth Flemming FM LM, Club Vice President

In the Autumn 2014 edition of The Kedge Anchor, *No 41, on pages 20 and 21, this was printed:*

In a very successful and ongoing relationship with The Milford-on-Sea Historical Record Society (MoSHRS) representatives of the Club met with key members of their committee in the Westover Churchill Room, Milford- on-Sea on 17 October, 2014.

The meeting was arranged to discuss the conservation and celebration of the discovery of Admiral Cornwallis' grave site as well as the restoration of the monuments of Admirals John Peyton and

Robert Man in All Saints Church, Milford-on-Sea.

Various ideas were discussed on how to con- serve the grave site of Admiral Cornwallis which also contains his flag captain John Whitby RN and his wife Mary Ann Theresa. The top of the grave is cracked and appears to have been completely broken while the inscription is becoming illegible by erosion and algae growth. The inscription only records John Whitby RN and is his original marker which has been moved to its present location. It is entirely in keeping with Cornwallis's wishes that "he was to be buried with his flag captain and that no memorial is be raised to him"; in compliance, neither does the stone record Mary Ann Theresa Whitby.

The general opinion was to minimise the work on the Cornwallis/ Whitby grave in accordance with the Club's Conservation Guidelines, to recommend to Council a formal survey to con- firm this, and to place a plaque to the east of the grave on the nearby

costings for the restoration work and to discuss the proposals with the church officials. They will then contact The 1805 Club with a suggested plan of actions, financing and timing.

Mr Jim Butterworth, secretary to the MoSHRS says, "The objectives of the proposal are to show the general public some of the historically important naval aspects of our village and to emphasise the immense contribution which these three men and many others from our village have made, at great personal cost, in the defence of our realm giving us the freedom which we enjoy today".

The monument to Admiral John Goodwin Gregory Peyton within All Saints Church is clearly in need of restoration and some small conservation. It would be a fitting example if

wall, with a copy of the grave inscription along with the Admiral's burial details. These suggestions will be presented to Council for discussion in time for its November meeting.

It was further thought that a plaque could be placed to the left of the Cornwallis Monument on the north wall inside the church with more details of his naval exploits in the protection of our isles against invasion and to include details of the collaborative conservation/restoration project between both organisations.

The Peyton wall mounted memorial above the organ loft has suffered greatly. Some of the appendages have come loose and are stacked on the organ loft roof. It is not thought difficult to restore this monument which has a good explanation of Admiral Peyton's exploits at the battle of the Nile. The brass marker of his grave in the central aisle of the nave is in reasonable condition requiring only minor conservation.

It was agreed that the group should produce a document for the general public outlining the very important contributions the three men made and their association with Admiral Lord Nelson, to be available within the church.

The MoSHRS volunteered to obtain

a memorial to one of Nelson's Nile Captain's was brought back to its original appearance using the original stone work.

John Peyton married Susanna Gurnell, widow, nee Swindon, daughter of the Rev Samuel Francis Swindon, Rector of Greenwich. In a letter written onboard HMS *Defence* off the Nile and dated 13 August, 1798 he says;

"I find myself a stouter man since the action, another such would make me a fine young fellow. God bless you".

Oliver Warner says of Peyton's action at the Nile. "Not a moment was lost; not a break for recovery. It is no wonder that the Band of Brothers were invincible".

The grave marker of Admiral Man in the choir vestry entry is in good condition and requires only cleaning and a plaque nearby to explain his naval exploits. At the time of Rigaud's painting Man did fine work on HMS *Cerberus* when he fell in with the Spanish fleet consisting of twelve sail of the line and several frigates under Don Joseph Solano. He followed the Spanish for several days, proceed- ing to give the earliest intelligence dispatches to Admiral Sir George Rodney, whom he found at anchor at Barbados. On 28 February 1781 off Cape Finisterre he captured the Spanish 28 gun *Graña*, under Don Nicolás de Medina. The Spanish had seven killed and seventeen wounded while *Cerberus* had two wounded. He was promoted to Admiral of the Blue on July 4 1794 and raised his flag on HMS *Defence* (Peyton's command at the Nile). After being promoted to Admiral of the White he transferred his flag to HMS *Victory* on 7 July, 1795 and took part in the the Battle of Hyères Islands on 13 July, 1795. *Victory* suffered considerable damage, having had her stays shot away, as well as much of the rigging. When in command of a detached squadron at Gibraltar in 1796 his judgment ran out when instead of supplying Admiral Sir John Jervis's blockading fleet off Toulon he returned to England to refit.

Jervis was infuriated and scapegoated Man, who was nonetheless appointed to one of the Lords Commisioners of the Admiraltity in 1798. By seniority he was promoted to Admiral of the Red on 12 August 1812. 🐦

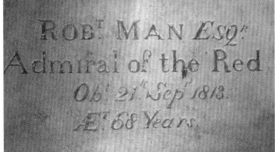

Early Notification of a Key Club Event for Next Year – 5 to 7 July 2019
COMMEMORATION OF THE DEATH OF ADMIRAL SIR WILLIAM CORNWALLIS G.C.B. 200 YEARS AGO AT MILFORD-ON-SEA, HAMPSHIRE
Stephen Tregidgo Member representing the Club on the Organising Committee.

In Spring 2018 Issue No 49 of The Kedge Anchor, *this event was announced:*

Milford-on-Sea is a large village parish of just under 5,000 on the outskirts of the New Forest. For such a small place it is a wonder that its church is the resting place of not just one Admiral from Napoleonic times, but of three. Cornwallis, Peyton and Man are all buried here and on 5th July 2019, it will be exactly 200 years ago to the day that Admiral Sir William Cornwallis died. His home was Newlands, an estate at Milford-on-Sea, part of which is now the South Lawn Hotel, which The 1805 Club will be using as its base for the 200th Commemoration events (more of which later).

Additionally to Milford-on-Sea, the wider area has many links to the Georgian sailing navy that have been brought together as part of a Heritage Trail. This includes:

- Bucklers Hard which was the dockyard that produced a number of Georgian sailing men-of-war including Nelson's favourite, the *Agamemnon*;
- Admiral Sir Harry Neale (born Harry Burrard, but changed his name on marriage) lived and is buried in nearby Lymington (Burrard Inlet in Vancouver Bay is named after him - as is Burrard Street and Burrard Bridge in Vancouver, named before he changed his name);
- The New Forest which produced many of the trees used in building the 'Wooden Walls' of the British Navy;
- Hurst Castle which guards the west entrance to The Solent between the New Forest and the Isle of Wight.

Enough of the wider area for the moment though, as it is Admiral Cornwallis who is the main subject of this article. He was the younger brother of Charles Cornwallis, the 1st Marquis Cornwallis, who was the British Army Commander who surrendered the British Army at the Battle of Yorktown in 1781. William joined the navy in 1755 aged 11. His illustrious 50-year naval career spanned no less than four major wars – the Seven Years War with France – the American Revolutionary War with America and France – the Third Anglo-Mysore War with Tipu Sultan (aided by France) – and last but not least the French Revolutionary War. It was in the latter that Cornwallis was the Commander-in-Chief of the Channel Fleet from 1801 to 1806.

1803 to 1805 became the period known as The Trafalgar Campaign where the British strategic principle was to prevent an invading French fleet from both forming and, if it did crossing the Channel. Cornwallis' Channel fleet was therefore an essential, key element of the strategy. Tasked directly with ensuring Vice-Admiral Gantaeume and his fleet did not venture out of Brest, Cornwallis kept him bottled up in the port for 3 years. Through careful disposition of the Channel fleet and excellent handling of ensuring effective victualing, Cornwallis demonstrated all the best qualities of a fleet commander. It was his fleet that prevented Villeneuve, on his dash across the Atlantic from the West Indies, meeting with Gantaeume and gaining any French control of the Channel to enable Napoleon's assembled land forces at Boulougne to invade Britain.

As everyone knows, the Trafalgar Campaign ended with the comprehensive defeat of the Combined French and Spanish fleets at the battle of the Campaign name and provided Nelson with his Immortal fame. Nelson, had he lived, would have been one of the first to recognise the consummate fleet commander skills displayed by his friend Cornwallis - all so adeptly applied in the Channel. Further,

Nelson would have acknowledged Cornwallis' success in preventing Villeneuve access to the Channel as being the necessary pre-requisite to setting up the culminating battle.

It was with the Trafalgar campaign background, not to mention Cornwallis' half a century's service to the Royal Navy, that The 1805 Club has joined the Milford-on-Sea Historical Record Society (MoSHRS) to plan a long weekend of events to commemorate the 200th anniversary of Cornwallis's death. The support from the Club to MoSHRS began in 2014 when founder members Keith Evans and Ken Flemming made contact with the vicar of All Saints, Milford as to the possible site of Admiral William Cornwallis's grave. At the time, it was unknown and uncertain if it was even at Milford. The vicar passed the query to the MoSHRS and initial contact was made introducing the Club and its interest in establishing that the site was there, even if it lay unrecognized.

After considerable research the vault was located very close to the north side of the church tower. It was found to have been moved in the late Victorian era to accommodate, in addition to Cornwallis himself, his flag Captain, John Whitby RN and his wife Mary Anne Theresa. Discussions began both on raising funds and also with the church authorities on how to approach their increasingly complicated procedures with regard to conservation of graves and other naval memorials within the church. One major issue was the need to restore and re-site the disintegrated Admiral Peyton memorial that had lain on the organ roof out of sight for many years. After several meetings and much research over the next 3 years the new site was established before full Club involvement was sought. It was always the intention that the Club should be a partner supporting MoSHRS in the funding and conservation programme. Discussions with the church stonemason Hoare Banks Stonemasons of Bournemouth, led by MoSHRS produced excellent competitive results over costings allowing the programme to proceed with the costs being absorbed by both organisations. This allowed full restoration to be completed on time and well before the 200th anniversary thanks to the splendid efforts of MoSHRS.

Our Chair and Vice-Chair, Peter Warwick and Bill White, met with MoSHRS members early in 2017 to discuss ideas on how the Club might support MoSHRS in the commemorations. As a Club member living near Portsmouth, Peter asked me if I would be willing to be the Club's link to MoSHRS given my physical proximity to Milford. Agreeing, my first meeting with Chris Hobby, MoSHRS Chair, was at Milford-on-Sea on a beautiful sunny, autumn day in October 2017. Chris first of all showed me around Milford's All Saints Church where the Commemoration service will be held. It is a wonderful picturesque church with its memorials to Admirals Peyton and Man being inside the church. Cornwallis is buried, together with his Flag Captain, John Whitby and John Whitby's wife, Mary Anne Theresa under a simple stone outside in the churchyard. A 'simple stone', because Cornwallis himself requested no fuss be made of him, shunning as he did all publicity about himself. We left the church to have lunch at the South Lawn Hotel, part of which is of an original building of Cornwallis' Newlands estate. There is a Conference/Ball Room at the hotel aptly named the Cornwallis Suite and it is here that I felt the Commemoration dinner on Saturday 6 July 2019 should be held.

MoSHRS have established a planning Committee for the Commemoration weekend. I attend as the Club's representative. Early planning has it that the Trafalgar Way horse-driven post-chaise will set things off by arriving at the church prior to the Commemoration Service starting at 1400 on Friday 5 July 2019. Plans are to include a Sea Cadets guard of honour presence at which the Bishop of Basingstoke

will be present alongside other dignitaries including officials of MoSHRS and of The 1805 Club, serving officers of the Royal Navy and others. At the conclusion of the service, guests will process to the village green where a series of events, all in outline at present, will take place. This may include a band, a naval presentation, a barbecue - all are in the very initial discussion/planning stages as this is written. On Saturday 6th July, initial plans are to visit the Heritage Trail sites of the area (see above), which would include Bucklers Hard. There will be a Commemoration dinner at the Cornwallis Suite, South Lawn Hotel at which Professor Andrew Lambert has agreed to be our Speaker. On Sunday 7th July there may be a visit planned for the morning with a conclusion to the events being at lunchtime.

The Club is reserving The South Lawn Hotel for those members who want to stay for the weekend. More details about booking and so on will be forthcoming nearer the time. For now, members either thinking they might want to come or know they will want to, are requested to note the dates in their diaries for now - Friday 5th July to Sunday 7th July 2019. It will not go unnoticed by North American or Canadian members the historical links between the Milford-on-Sea wider area with those countries. Admiral Cornwallis' brother surrendered the British forces at Yorktown and Admiral Sir Harry Neale, buried in Lymington, gave his name to sites around Vancouver. This therefore makes the event of particular interest to those 'across the pond'! If you are able to make it you are ensured a very warm welcome (although we cannot guarantee the weather, we will do our best!). I hope to see you.

Note:
Details of Admiral Cornwallis, his Newlands estate, John Whitby RN and Mary Ann Theresa Whitby can be found in The *Kedge Anchor* Issue 40. Summer 2014. Pages 1, 4, 5, 6 and 7. ✒

CORNWALLIS AND WHITBY GRAVE UPDATE
By Stephen Tregidgo

In the Autumn 2018 Issue 50 of The Kedge Anchor *there was a note on page 31:*

The turf around the grave had suffered from the hot, dry summer and the feet of the contractors replacing the window above it. Consequently the grass was removed and replaced with shingle. While a small information plaque was also put into place.

Admiral Sir William Cornwallis GCB
20 February 1744-5 July 1819
Captain John Whitby
7 October 1774-7 April 1806
Mary Anne Theresa Whitby
18 December 1783-5 August 1850
Erected by
Milford-on-Sea Historical Record Society
and The 1805 Club

NOTICE OF CLUB EVENT JULY 2019

On the centre pages in the previous Spring 2018 edition of *The Kedge Anchor,* I had written an article notifying members of early plans for an event in Milford-on-Sea, Hampshire in the New Forest. The event is to commemorate the 200th anniversary of the death of Admiral Sir William Cornwallis. The Admiral lived in Milford and is buried in the grounds of its All Saints Church.

Taking place over the long weekend of Friday July 5th to Sunday July 7th 2019, the event is being led by the Milford- on-Sea Historical Record Society (MoSHRS) with The 1805 Club as very active partners. All will start with a Commemoration service led by the Bishop of Basingstoke at the church and be followed by:

- a re-enactment of the arrival of the Trafalgar Dispatch in the Trafalgar Way Post Chaise,
- a procession to the village green for refreshments and entertainment,
- a visit on the Saturday to Bucklers Hard and its museum dockyard where Nelson's favourite ship HMS *Agamemnon* was built
- a Commemoration dinner at the South Lawn Hotel which was part of Cornwallis' home and which is reserved for the accommodation of those members wishing to stay.
- Professor Andrew Lambert will be the guest speaker.
- a visit on the Sunday to St Barbe's museum in nearby Lymington which will be hosting a Summer Exhibition on Cornwallis and the area's extensive links with Georgian sailing navy,
- a Heritage Trail for those wishing to find out more about the area's links with the sailing navy.

Plans are now advancing well and expressions of interest from members have been requested to aid planning. For more information, I would refer you back to the last edition.

There will be more details and invitations to the event in the New Year

THE PRE-HISTORY OF THE COLLABORATION BETWEEN MILFORD-ON-SEA HISTORICAL RECORD SOCIETY AND The 1805 Club
By Barry Jolly

When I retired some two decades ago, I spent the best part of a decade as a volunteer room steward with the National Trust at Sizergh Castle in the old county of Westmoreland. The history of the property and of the Strickland family – resident since the mid-thirteenth century – seemed to me to be in need of revision, and, after some years of research I decided to pen some notes for my colleagues on the wonderful collection of family and royal portraits on display.

However, I was somewhat bemused by two portraits – of a naval captain and his wife, John and Theresa Whitby – which did not seem to fit the situation, so much so that the two paragraph limit per portrait I had set myself was soon exhausted, and a small volume of some 96 pages emerged.

I had previously been sent two old copies of the Milford-on-Sea Historical Record Society *Occasional Magazine,* with articles on 'The Making of Mrs Whitby' and 'The Story of Newlands Manor', and so the logical place for publication was Milford-on-Sea itself. So it was that in 2011 the Society published 'Mrs Whitby's Locket: The story of Captain John Whitby England's youngest ever sea captain and his redoubtable wife' – a story which not only encompassed the relationship of John and Theresa Whitby in their different ways with Admiral Cornwallis, but was inextricably entwined with the last three and a half decades of Cornwallis' life.

[The eponymous locket was made for Mrs Whitby when her husband died. It was commissioned by Cornwallis himself, and is now in the Gilbert Collection at the Victoria and Albert Museum.]

A letter by the Admiral's brother, Earl Cornwallis, in 1804 illustrates the significance of the relationship:
The first grand faux pas that he made in '96, and this second mistake, which might have proved fatal for the future repose and comfort of his life, have both been occasioned by his attachment to Whitby, and his earnest desire to have him as Captain of his ship. What trifles direct the fortune of men whom nature has qualified to be great!

Two years after 'Mrs Whitby's Locket' was published, John Bewley asked his well-known question about the location of Cornwallis' grave, a grave now recognised as being well stocked with not just the Admiral, but with both the Whitbys plus their daughter and a grand-daughter to boot.

More articles have followed: 'Admiral Sir William Cornwallis - Aspects of a Life' in the Society's Cornwallis Bicentenary Edition of the *Occasional Magazine;* 'Cornwallis and Hampshire' in *Hampshire Studies*; 'Cornwallis, A Woman Named Cuba, and the Caribbean' in *The Trafalgar Chronicle*; 'Honouring Cornwallis' in *The Kedge Anchor* and 'The Three Admirals Window at Milford-on-Sea' in *The Glazier.*

The Society is proud not only of its decade long collaboration with The 1805 Club, but also of its contribution to research on the Admiral, both enabling and enhancing that collaboration.

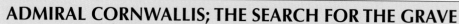

ADMIRAL CORNWALLIS; THE SEARCH FOR THE GRAVE
By Bob Braid, Trustee & Keeper of MoSHRS Archive

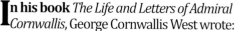

In his book *The Life and Letters of Admiral Cornwallis*, George Cornwallis West wrote:

> "He gave directions as to his funeral and that he was to be 'buried alongside his friend Captain John Whitby in Milford Churchyard,' also that no tombstone or memorial was to be erected to his memory. This last injunction Mrs Whitby obeyed to the letter. Her daughter, however, ignored it, for she not only built a family vault, to which she caused the coffins of her parents and the Admiral to be transferred, but also put up a large memorial tablet in the church itself………"

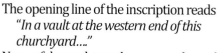

The opening line of the inscription reads
> "*In a vault at the western end of this churchyard….*"

None of the vaults on the western boundary of the churchyard could be identified as the one mentioned and, over the years, it became assumed that the vault was either unmarked in accordance with the admiral's wishes, or lost. The years 2014 & 2015 saw a series of happy coincidences. First, in 2014, Milford-on-Sea

Historical Record Society (MoSHRS) was contacted by 1805 Club Vice Presidents, Keith Evans and Ken Flemming, after an intervention at the Club Members' Day the previous year in which the loss of Cornwallis' grave was raised. Following a visit to Milford by Keith and Ken (reported in KA 39), members of MoSHRS decided it really was time that efforts were made to locate the grave.

A set of handwritten sheets was found in MoSHRS archive, the second of which contained a transcript of the inscription on John Whitby's grave. At about the same time, the editor of the society's newsletter happened to be in the churchyard late one afternoon when the lowering sun caught a ground-level grave slab at an angle so that she thought she could see 'John Whitby'. Subsequent investigation and comparison with the transcript confirmed that the slab was indeed that of John Whitby. The slab was broken in two and suffering from moisture damage and was at further risk from mowing operations (*picture below*).

The inscription reads:

In Memory of John Whitby Esq. Son of the Rev Thos Whitby of Cresswell Hall Staffordshire. Born the 7th of October 1774 He was promoted to the Rank of Post Captain in his Majesties Navy on the 20th of April 1793 and departed this life on the 7th of April 1806.

There followed a series of negotiations with the Church, the Parochial Church Council, the Diocese and stonemasons Hoare Banks over what could be done to conserve the slab and protect it from further damage. The conservation work was completed in 2018 and a stainless steel plaque, supplied by The 1805 Club, installed.

However, the story does not end there. After the commemoration event held on the 200th anniversary of Cornwallis' death in 2019, a newspaper report was found of the funeral of Theresa John Cornwallis West, Captain & Mrs Whitby's daughter, which said that she was interred in the family vault. Also, a check of the Parish Burial Registers revealed against the entry for Mrs West's youngest daughter a note *"Vault, old part"*. As a result, in 2021, a replacement plaque was installed incorporating the names of all five.

Perhaps finally, a matter of two weeks before the memorial stone dedication at Portsmouth, two photographs surfaced, taken before the construction of the choir vestry in 1933, which show (albeit not very clearly in the reduced copy attached) that originally the vault was surmounted by a chest tomb located slightly further away from the tower lean-to wall. It appears that, when the vestry was built, the chest was removed and the grave ledger moved to one side and set at ground level.

The original location of the burials of Captain Whitby and the Admiral has never been established. ⚓

THE NAVAL STAINED GLASS WINDOW
By Chris Hobby

The Naval Stained Glass Window is "dedicated to the memory of Admiral Sir William Cornwallis, Admiral Robert Man, Rear Admiral John Peyton and Captain John Whitby".

The majority of people associate stained glass works with churches, but Steve Sherriff, who produced our window, said that the majority of his company's work is traditional leaded lights usually into metal frames which are fitted either into wood or stone.

He was approached by the Reverend Dominic Furness, who at the time was incumbent at All Saints' Parish Church at Milford-on-Sea, to replace a stained glass window in the church and was given some broad parameters regarding its design. When designing a new stained glass window the initial design is done in black and white, and consideration has to be given to the traditional feel and history of the ancient church building. In Steve's own words "it's most important how it will sit amongst the other windows around it as it cannot shout its presence". That said, it will be a

modern window using the most up-to-date methods in its construction. Thus, the window would consist of traditional painting on glass and include some art glass which would go around the central ensign design to depict the sky, earth and sea.

The Red Ensign is very modern in the technique of its production as it is of fused glass, being a first for the company; the ripples in the glass are produced during the fusing process in the kiln, creating the appearance of the flag fluttering.

The basic design on paper took about a week, though any alterations, such as a change in a date or an inscription, meant that the design would have to be reworked to ensure that the perspective and everything else that has changed will sit well together; it is of paramount importance that one element does not dominate over another, the emphasis being the ensign and the names around it. Then of course, one must consider the colours involved, as all have to sit comfortably together.

Continued on page 67

CORNWALLIS REMEMBERED 5TH-7TH JULY 2019

By Kathy Brown

On 1 July 2019 The Trafalgar Way website announced the forthcoming celebrations at Milford-on-Sea:

The weekend of 5th to 7th July will be a celebration of a well-loved Naval hero in Milford-on-Sea in Hampshire.

Hampshire village Milford-on-Sea is host, this coming weekend, to a series of celebration events remembering the life of Admiral William Cornwallis (1744-1819). The 1805 Club has lent its support to the local history group, Milford-on-Sea Historical Record Society (MoSHRS) to plan a special set of events. A church ceremony on Friday 5th July will see the blessing of a new stained glass window commemorating three 'Admirals of the Red' who were contemporaries of Nelson and who are all buried in the pretty churchyard of All Saints in Milford.

A fascinating and little known fact about Admiral Cornwallis is that, in spite of his great achievements in protecting British shores, he was ultimately a very humble and unassuming man. He is buried in an unmarked grave. He insisted, in his last testament, that he be buried anonymously, with no memorial service or monument raised. This was perhaps ordained as a deliberate direct contrast to the funeral pomp following the death of Lord Nelson, which he possibly found somewhat distasteful, in spite of his great respect for his famous peer. In any case, Cornwallis ended up being interred alongside his friend and protégé, Captain John Whitby, who had died previously, in 1806. Cornwallis left his fortune to Whitby's widow, who had cared for him after the death of her own husband.

Immediately after the church ceremony on Friday afternoon there will be an enactment imagining the arrival of the Trafalgar dispatch in Milford-on-Sea, with a presentation to the Lord Lieutenant of Hampshire. The Trafalgar Way team are participating in this, with our costumed Lapenotiere arriving in the stunning yellow post-chaise outside the church at around 3.15pm, then continuing down to the village green at around 3.30pm for a second stop and presentation to local representatives. All are welcome to come along and witness this ever-memorable spectacle!

On the village green from 3pm until 5pm there will be a variety of themed entertainment and live music with The Trafalgar Way and Royal Navy stands providing information. Was YOUR ancestor at Trafalgar? Come along to ask us and consult the Trafalgar rolls on the spot! Refreshments will be provided by local village groups including the Primary School and Royal Navy Catering. Children from the local school, who will have enjoyed a "Wooden World" workshop courtesy of The 1805 Club earlier in the day, will put on a short and playful re-enactment of the Battle of Trafalgar. ⚓

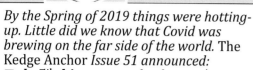

CORNWALLIS REMEMBERED WEEKEND
5TH–7TH July 2019
Invitation to The 1805 Club members
Alison Reijman, Geraint Day and Stephen Tregidgo

By the Spring of 2019 things were hotting-up. Little did we know that Covid was brewing on the far side of the world. The Kedge Anchor *Issue 51 announced:*

July 5th this year marks the 200th anniversary of the death of Admiral Sir William Cornwallis. Commander-in-Chief of the Channel Fleet between 1801 and 1806, who was a key figure in the Trafalgar Campaign and a great friend of Lord Nelson.

In 1800, Cornwallis made his home at the Newlands Estate in the Hampshire village of Milford-on-Sea, located on the edge of the New Forest. The village is the setting for a weekend of bicentenary commemorations and activities that the Milford-on-Sea Historical Record Society (MoSHRS) is organising in partnership with The 1805 Club from Friday 5 July to Sunday 7t July.

Our partner, MoSHRS is one of the oldest local history societies in the country. Founded in 1909, the Society has so far collected more than 8,000 historical records which it is making available through its online archive catalogue. The Cornwallis Bicentenary Project is one of its two current major activities and we will join its members during the weekend for a commemoration service, a visit to Buckler's Hard and a commemoration dinner.

Cornwallis was a key figure in the Royal Navy for 50 years. Joining the navy in 1755 aged 11, his illustrious career spanned four major wars – the Seven Years War with France, the American Revolutionary War with America and France, the Third Anglo-Mysore War with Tipu Sultan (aided by France) and the French Revolutionary War.

The period between 1803 and 1805 was known as the Trafalgar Campaign, the aim of which was to prevent an invading French fleet from both forming and consequently crossing the Channel. The Channel Fleet commanded by Cornwallis was therefore pivotal to the success of the strategy. Tasked directly with ensuring Vice-Admiral Gantaeume and his fleet did not venture out of Brest, Cornwallis kept him confined to port for three years.

It was Cornwallis' fleet that prevented Villeneuve, on his dash across the Atlantic from the West Indies, from meeting with Gantaeume, thereby halting any French control of the Channel that could have led to Napoleon's assembled land forces in Boulogne invading Britain.

The Trafalgar Campaign ended with the comprehensive defeat of the Combined French and Spanish fleets at the Battle of Trafalgar on 21 October 1805. Had Nelson lived, he would have undoubtedly been one of the first to recognise the outstanding skills and leadership displayed by Cornwallis during his command of the Channel.

Cornwallis also served as an MP, first for Eye, and later for Portsmouth. He leased the Newlands Estate in 1800, buying it later and living there until his death in 1819. Part of the estate is now the South Lawn Hotel, which will be The 1805 Club's base throughout the Cornwallis Remembered weekend.

This strikingly attractive hotel, located conveniently on the main road into Milford-on-Sea, is set in extensive peaceful grounds. Its centrepiece is the Cornwallis Suite where the commemorative dinner will be

held on the Saturday night.

Another feature is its Cedar Tree Restaurant, named after the huge cedar tree in its grounds, which offers reasonably priced two or three course menus, together with an à la carte menu.

Milford-on-Sea is a picturesque village renowned for its long stretch of shingle beach commanding outstanding views across the Solent to the Isle of Wight and the Needles. It is also close to the fishing village of Keyhaven, whose long shingle bank leads to Hurst Castle, Henry VIII's artillery fort built to protect against invasion from France and the Holy Roman Empire.

The village church, All Saints', is also the final resting place of not just Cornwallis, but two other admirals from Napoleonic times, Admiral Robert Man and Rear Admiral John Peyton. Our location for the weekend is also an excellent gateway to the beautiful, world-renowned New Forest, William the Conquer- or's hunting ground which is now a National Park, rich in natural and cultural history, and famous for its native ponies. The New Forest was also responsible for providing thousands of trees to build the "Wooden Walls" of the Royal Navy.

Within the New Forest are two of the other fascinating places we shall be visiting during the weekend. One is the unique hamlet of Buckler's Hard set within the Beaulieu Estate where ships were built for Nelson's fleet at Trafalgar including his favourite, HMS *Agamemnon*.

The Maritime Museum tells the story of Buckler's Hard while historic displays in the Labourer's and Shipwright's cottages show how the village would have looked in the early 1800s. The visit to Buckler's Hard also includes a boat trip along the picturesque, tranquil Beaulieu River, one of the few privately owned rivers in the world.

There will also be an opportunity to visit vibrant Lymington, an ancient seaport, well-known historically for its salt mak- ing and ship building, which is now a popular yachting cen- tre. It is also the final resting place of Admiral Sir Harry Neale, who gave his name to sites around Vancou- ver. The town's St Barbe Museum and Art Gallery tells the story of the town from William the Conqueror to the Second World War. Currently, it is also the venue for an exhibition, Command of the Seas!

The weekend itinerary: Friday 5 July 2019

The weekend will start with a Commemoration Service at All Saints' Church, Milford-on-Sea on Friday 5th July at 14.00, conducted by the Bishop of Basingstoke, the Rt Rev David Williams. It will be attended by officials from The 1805 Club and MoSHRS, and serving Royal Navy officers, while local Sea Cadets will provide

a guard of honour. The Cornwallis grave and Peyton memorial will be re-dedicated and a new stained glass window at the church commemorating the three Milford admirals will be blessed. The post- chaise, used for the New Trafalgar Dispatch and now by the Trafalgar Way, will also visit the church.

After the service, the congregation will process to the village green for a series of celebration events, which will include the post-chaise, live music, Trafalgar Way and Royal Navy stands, with refreshments provided by local organisations including the primary school and Royal Navy Catering.

The evening is free for members to relax in the hotel, dine at the Cedar Tree Restaurant or other local restaurants, a list of which will be made available prior to the weekend.

Saturday 6 July

Breakfast at the hotel will be followed by a visit to Buckler's Hard by coach. Members of both The 1805 Club and MoSHRS will be able to visit all the attractions at the village and take a boat trip along the Beaulieu River. Allocated time slots will be made for the boat trip and entry to the Museum. There is a choice of places to eat and drink, including the Master Builder Hotel and the Captain's Cabin Tea Room, which members can enjoy at their leisure.

The coach will pick members up by 16.30 giving members ample time to prepare for the Commemorative Dinner which starts at 19.00 at which members of MoSHRS will again be joining us in the Cornwallis Suite. Dress code for dinner will be black tie or lounge suit for men with equivalent attire for ladies.

Following a welcome reception hosted by the hotel and introduction from The 1805 Club and MoSHRS Chairmen, there will be a three course meal. This will

comprise: - starters, smoked salmon & prawn rillette, fennel, cucumber & lemon crème fraiche; main course, braised Hampshire beef steak bourguignon, herb mash & seasonal vegetables; dessert, summer pudding with clotted cream ice cream – all followed by freshly brewed coffee & after dinner mints. The dinner will be served with three glasses of wine and a glass of port. There will then be an address by a guest speaker on the life of Cornwallis. The evening will conclude with a cash bar.

Sunday 7 July

Members can visit the Command of the Seas! Exhibition at the St Barbe Museum and Art Gallery in Lymington in the morning before the conclusion of the weekend or explore more of the New Forest at leisure before returning home.

For members only wishing to stay one night or would prefer to stay elsewhere in the area, the following accommodation is available.

The Beach House, Cliff Road, Milford-on-Sea, tel: 01590 64344. Website: https:// www.beachhousemilfordonsea.co.uk/

Harvest House B&B, Lymington Road, Milford-on-Sea, tel: 01590 644579. Website: https://harvesthousenewforest.co.uk/

Vinegar Hill Pottery B&B, Mockbeggars, Vinegar Hill, Milford-on-Sea, tel: 01590 642979. Website: https://www.vinegarhillpottery.co.uk/

The Marine B&B, Hurst Road, Milford-on-Sea, tel: 01590 644369. Website: https:// www.marinehousebnb.co.uk/

Dee's B&B, 2 Knowland Drive, Milford-on-Sea, tel: 01590 645494. Website: http:/ /www.deesbnb.co.uk/

Accommodation in the wider area can also be searched and booked through the tourist board - Go New Forest: https:// www.thenewforest.co.uk/accommodation

CORNWALLIS REMEMBERED:
THE COMMEMORATION CELEBRATIONS 5-7 JULY 2019

The big weekend in Milford-on-Sea was reported in The Kedge Anchor *Issue 52, in the Autumn of 2019, reproduced here on pages 41-56:*

Nigel Atkinson Esq HM Lord-Lieutenant of Hampshire lays a wreath on the grave of Admiral Sir William Cornwallis GCB his Flag

Captain John Whitby RN and Mary Ann Theresa Whitby. During a commemorative service in All Saints' church Milford-on-Sea, to mark the bi-centenary of the death of Admiral The Honourable Sir William Cornwallis, and to honour two other admirals commemorated within the church who secured the freedom of the seas in the wars against France 1793-1815

This joint event took place over the 5-6-7 July 2019 at Milford-on-Sea, Hampshire The 1805 Club joining with The Milford-on-Sea Historical Record Society (MoSHRS) over the three-day event after 6 years of joint planning and restoration efforts.

A question had been asked by member John Bewley at the May 2013 AGM did we the Club know the Cornwallis gravesite; thought to be at Milford, where the Admiral had lived after his retirement [*Note: this statement of John Bewley's question was incorrect, and has subsequently been corrected by John. The actual question was that he knew of no national monument to Cornwallis and proposed the The 1805 Club investigate.*] The late Carol Evans, wife of Vice President Keith Evans wrote to the incumbent vicar who did not have any knowledge of the grave or even if it was located at Milford but happily passed the request to the Society.

A meeting was arranged by Milford Society member Jim Butterworth at All Saints Church, Milford on 26 October 2013. Where Vice Presidents Keith Evans and Kenneth Flemming introduced themselves and the Club and offered assistance to help locate the grave and possible restoration of the memorials. It was recognised at the outset the venture would be an outstanding achievement and event for both groups. This was the start of an exceptional relationship within two professional organisations working in full agreement to restore, safeguard and maintain, sites and memorials; not only important to the people of Milford, including the New Forest National Park but, also to National and Naval History. A further Club consideration is to raise a memorial plaque to Admiral Cornwallis within St Paul's Cathedral, London.

It had been acknowledged at this first meeting that a naval contingent including VIP guests would be highly attractive to support this national and international event. While also

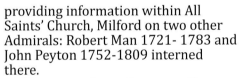

providing information within All Saints' Church, Milford on two other Admirals: Robert Man 1721- 1783 and John Peyton 1752-1809 interned there.

After several meetings over the primary 3 years the group had pin pointed the Cornwallis/Whitby gravesite [summarised in issue 40 summer 2014 of, *The Kedge Anchor*: *Two Remarkable People Rediscovered*.] and then planned the financial expenditure needed to repair and clean the grave ledger and to restore and re-hang the memorial to Admiral Robert Man (1745-1813). Meetings took place with the church authorities and stonemasons to discuss details and joint authorizations for the work to be carried out.

All were considered; before Club Council and involvement was sought. A report was passed to council to

study the objectives and the shared fiscal implications and conservation responsibilities of the proposed project. Full Club commitment was given by the late Chairman Peter Warwick.

Over a further period of 2 years local Club member Stephen Tregidgo took up the formidable challenge of organising and coordinating events while working on the MoSHRS planning committee for the Commemoration Celebrations. Their efforts and Stephen's steward- ship at the official dinner greatly enhanced an outstanding Club achievement.

The whole conservation work and events programme came under the combined guidance of Milford Society Chairman Chris Hobby and The 1805 Club.

Distinguished Guests attending the Celebrations:

The Rt Hon. The Earl Howe, Deputy Leader of the House of Lords and Former Minister of State for Defence and Countess Elizabeth Howe.

The 1805 Club President. Former First Sea Lord Admiral Sir Jonathon Band GCB DL, and Lady Sarah Band.

Rear Admiral Tim Hodgson MBE RN, Submarine Capability Ministry of Defence.

Commodore David Elford OBE ADC RN Naval Regional Commander Eastern England.

Nigel Atkinson Esq HM Lord-Lieutenant of Hampshire.

The RN display unit was commanded by Lt M Paterson, SO3 Engagement East Central England, Naval Regional Command Eastern England.

Also, representing the Navy:
Lt Cdr Jason Allen RN, OIC Victory

Squadron, HMS *Collingwood*. Lt Luke Haddon RN, HMS *Sultan*.
Lt David Vail RN, Commanding Officer HMS *Trumpeter.*

HMS *Collingwood* is the Royal Navy's largest Training Establishment. It is the headquarters of the Maritime Warfare School and Surface Stream which also has units in HM Training Establishments, Excellent, Longmoor, Temeraire, Horsea Island and Raleigh, delivering training in Warfare, Weapon Engineering, Diving, Physical Training, Chemical Biological Radiation Nuclear and Damage Control, Sea Survival, Seamanship and Military skills.

HMS *Sultan* Training Establishment.

The Marine Engineering department delivers all ME General Service and Submarine specialisation career course and pre-joining training. Headed by Commander Marine Engineering, the department consists of over 150 personnel spanning from RN officers and Senior Rates, to civilian and RFA in- structors all of whom support the department's four functional groups.

The Craft Skills Group – This group is charged with the delivery of basic and advanced craft skills, primarily to Marine Engineering officers and ratings.

In addition, the DSMarE work closely with the Nuclear Department to generate the delivery of all Marine Engineering General Service and Nuclear Sub- marine career and specialist training.

Having been summoned by a Full Peal of Bells taking 3 hours to achieve in the morning the Church was full for the Commemoration Service.

While guests arrived and became seated at 1330 the organist Timothy Rice played:
Carillon (Herbert Murrill)
Prelude in (G BWV 541, JS Bach) Prelude in Classic Style (Gordon Young) Hornpipe from The Water Music (GF Handel) Fugue in E flat "St Anne" (JS Bach) Solemn Melody (H Walford Davies)

At 1350 followed a Private Service for the Rededication of the Admiral Sir William Cornwallis and Captain John Whitby RN Ledger. Attending were; Richard Cornwallis, son of

Commander Michael Cornwallis (next in line), age 94. Descended from Cornwallis' brother, James, the Bishop of Lichfield. Next are Peter Mills and his wife, Karen. He is descended from Charlotte, one of the admiral's sisters. The last two are Julia Wykeham Martin and Lavinia Cartwright, both also descended from James, the Bishop.

Ensigns and Standard were brought forward after the Sunset was sounded by Bugler Bandsman Mike Thomas, Band of HM Royal Marines, Portsmouth at the Laying of the wreath followed by the Alert.

Singing of the 1st Hymn *All people that on earth do dwell* and were received by Revd Dominic Furness there followed:

A Tribute To The Three Admirals. Read by the Lord Lieutenant's Cadet. Rebecca Lee.

'On the two hundredth anniversary of the death of the Honourable Sir William Cornwallis, Admiral of the Red, let us hear the words of his god-daughter, Mrs Theresa West:

He was God's noblest work—a man upright, By grovelling minds but little understood; Benevolent as brave, most just, most true, Most good!

Revered by Nelson, and adored by his crews, Cornwallis spent his last nineteen years on earth in Milford, and is buried, at his own request, next to his protégé and good friend Captain John Whitby, in an unmarked grave. It is that grave which has been conserved and is the subject of

today's service. Cornwallis came to Milford in the footsteps of an old friend, Robert Man, Admiral of the Red. Nelson called him, *a good man in every sense of the word,* and he served his country well, both at sea and as a Lord Commissioner of the Admiralty directing the operations of the fleets of the Royal Navy across the world in the fight against Revolutionary France. Man was an active member of the congregation of this church. His grave-stone, set between the nave and the vestry, is simple in accordance with his own wishes, a mark of modesty of a man who also deserves our deepest respect. Many years after the Battle of The Nile, the first of Nelson's famous victories, Nelson wrote to one of his Band of Brothers, John Peyton, *It was never in my power to shew you those attentions which in every way your conduct entitled you to.* The faded memorial in this church to John Peyton, Rear Admiral of the Red, once lost behind the organ loft, symbolises an obscurity which has now been remedied. The conserved memorial now stands proudly and prominently in the choir.

We honour each of these courageous men whose long years at sea secured the freedom of our land.'

Followed by the Choir: *Sunset and Evening Star* (Parry) Bible reading 2 Timothy 4 v 1-8. Read by Peter Main, Headteacher Priestlands School, Lymington. Priestlands was the home of Admiral Peyton, now incorporated in the campus of the school.

Dedication of the Rear Admiral John Peyton Memorial by Chaplain Bernard Clarke RNR

'Today we remember the bravery and sacrifice of Admiral John Peyton who responded to the call to serve his country in a time of war and was one Nelson's Band of Brothers. This memorial is a reminder to us of bravery and courage under fire, but it also compels us to look forward; to

in his service."

The Naval Prayer read by Gillian Peard.

Eternal Lord God, Who alone spreadest out the heavens and rulest the raging of the seas; who hast compassed the waters with bounds until day and night come to an end: be pleased to receive into thy almighty and most gracious protection the persons of us thy servants and the fleet in which we serve. Preserve us from the dangers of the sea and of the air and from the violence of the enemy: that we may be safeguard unto our most sovereign lady, Queen Elizabeth, and her dominions, and a security for such as pass on the seas upon their lawful occasions; that the inhabitants of our island and commonwealth may in peace and quiet- ness serve thee our God; and that we may return in safety to enjoy the blessings of the land, with fruits of our labours and with a thankful remembrance of thy mercies to praise and glorify thy holy name; through Jesus Christ our Lord. Amen

First published in 1662 in the Book of

honour all who serve by seeking to build a better future. So, as we look back in remembrance of his leadership in command, his bravery and sacrifice, we also bear the responsibility of looking forward, look- ing ahead to ensure that the courage and sacrifice of others will never have been in vain, but rather that it offers new hope and opportunity to those who come after.'

There followed the Dedication of the New MoSHRS by Rt Revd David Williams, Bishop of Basingstoke.

"We dedicate this window to the glory of God and in the memory of Admiral Sir William Cornwallis; Rear Admiral John Peyton; Admiral Robert Man and Captain John Whitby. We thank you for their gifts and skills of seamanship, leadership, ser- vice and sacrifice. We pray that this window may beautify and make glorious this place of worship and inspire God's people to the remembrance of all who have lived and died

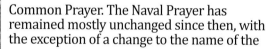

Common Prayer. The Naval Prayer has remained mostly unchanged since then, with the exception of a change to the name of the monarch, the change from "Empire" to "Commonwealth", a more recent deletion of the phrase "though Jesus Christ our Lord near the end."

The bugler gave the General Salute. There followed The National Anthem to conclude the service. 🔱

CORNWALLIS REMEMBERED

was a co-operative venture between Milford-on-Sea Historical Record Society,

The 1805 Club,

The New Forest National Park Authority and

The St Barbe Museum and Art Gallery.

It was further supported by donations from Hampshire Archives Trust, Hampshire County Council, Hampshire Field Club, Heritage Lottery Fund, Milford-on-Sea Parish Council, New Forest District Council, as well as many other local history groups and individual donations.

CELEBRATIONS CONTINUED ON MILFORD VILLAGE GREEN

COMMENTS ON THE EVENT

The Rt Hon. Earl Howe, who members will remember was the Guest of Honour at the Club's Trafalgar Dinner at HMS Nelson 2018, says of the event:

On 5th July, at All Saints Church, Milford-on-Sea, I was privileged to attend the beautifully scripted Commemoration service – long in the planning – marking the bicentenary of the death of Admiral Sir William Cornwallis, whose un-marked grave lies just outside the west door of the church.

It was a remarkable occasion, for more reasons than one; but chiefly for the recognition that it signalled for a naval figure whose contribution to the security – and some would argue, the survival – of our country has only recently been fully appreciated. Cornwallis, acknowledged by his early nineteenth century peers as having played a pivotal role in the wars against France, is no longer a household name, yet without his consummate command of the Channel Fleet between 1801 and 1805 it is almost certain that Napoleon's plans for the invasion of the United Kingdom would have reached fruition.

The very fitting tribute in the parish church was followed by further community celebrations on the village green. These included the dramatic arrival of a post-chaise containing a "messenger" bearing the news of Nelson's victory at Trafalgar – a telling reminder of the historical context of Cornwallis's achievements and of how much depended on the skill and dedication of our great naval commanders of that era.

The 1805 Club President. Former First Sea Lord Admiral Sir Jonathon Band also comments on the occasion. "Nothing beats an English village on a summer's day and so true that was when we celebrated the bicentenary of one of our great Georgian period admirals in Milford-on-Sea. It was an event of style and grace that befitted Cornwallis who secured the Channel against invasion and bottled up the French in their harbours. He set many of the conditions for Nelson's subsequent victory at Trafalgar."

Sir Jonathon adds:

"The 1805 Club were honoured to be involved."

ADMIRAL CORNWALLIS AND HMS *PICKLE*
By Chris Sanders

The preparation of this article has been greatly assisted by reference to *"HMS Pickle The Swiftest Ship in Nelson's Trafalgar Fleet"* by Peter Hore, The History Press 2015 as well as the website www.thetrafalgarway.org/hm-schooner-pickle.

At 12.30 on Thursday 4 July 2019, HMS *Pickle* manoeuvred up the Lymington River to moor. She was later joined by HMS *Trumpeter*.

with a crew of 35. She had three main roles: carrying despatches between her fleet and the Admiralty; inshore work from close observation of the enemy to interception of the enemy's coastal craft; and finally rescue when ships got into difficulties.

Britain declared war (again) on 18 May 1803. Ten sail of the line and some frigates sailed immediately from Crawsand with orders to cruise off Ushant and watch the

Both vessels were present to mark the commemoration of Admiral Cornwallis the following day. *HMS Trumpeter* (P294) is an Archer-class patrol vessel P2000-type patrol and training vessel of the Royal Navy. *Pickle* is a "pretty accurate lookalike of the original turn-of-the-19th-century Pickle ... blessed with a motor as well as authentic sails." The opportunity was taken to distribute leaflets promoting the exhibition "Command of the Seas: The Navy and the New Forest against Napoleon" which was running at the St Barbe Museum and Art Gallery, Lymington from 6th June until 1st September.

The real *Pickle* in the Royal Navy of the early Nineteenth Century was a schooner

activities of the French ships in Brest Harbour. The Channel Fleet, to which *Pickle* was attached, was under Admiral Cornwallis, its Commander-in-Chief.

Cornwallis faced many requests for small ships and *Pickle* was sent to join Collingwood's inshore squadron to be used in intercepting the small vessels along the coast. She then resumed her duties, next delivering dispatches from Cornwallis urging the Admiralty to send more small ships: "A stout armed cutter is very much wanted to be with the inshore ships, the *Pickle* schooner having been constantly on that service." Meanwhile *Pickle* had been into Brest Roads to count the ships there, and Collingwood wrote to Cornwallis: 'The

Pickle this morning at daylight, when it was very clear, and objects seen clearly, so that I believe every vessel in the port is enumerated in the *Pickle*'s list.'

The following year, *Pickle* was able to aid damaged and stricken ships in Cornwallis' fleet such as *Atalante* and *Magnificent*. *Pickle*'s work did not stop, and over the coming months she made several fast voyages between Plymouth and the ships of the Channel fleet.

Cornwallis and the fleet had come to rely on *Pickle*, dependable, quick and ready to serve. So it was a disgruntled Cornwallis who complained to the Admiralty on 7 February 1805 about the need for more dispatch vessels to carry the orders between his ships and Plymouth and, in particular, at the redeployment of one of the little workhorses of his fleet. He grumbled that 'the *Pickle*, armed schooner, which I had stationed there [off Ferrol], had upon her putting into Plymouth ... [been] away upon some other service'.

Pickle first served in the West Indies then returned to join Nelson's fleet at Trafalgar.

Five days after the Battle of Trafalgar in October 1805, Vice Admiral Collingwood ordered Lt Lapenotiere, who commanded the *Pickle,* to sail England and deliver his Dispatch to the Admiralty.

On 5th July 2019, an actor in a post-chaise visited Milford-on-Sea. "Lieutenant Lapenotiere" delivered his message "We have gained a great victory, but we have lost Lord Nelson" first, to the congregation leaving All Saints Church following the service of commemoration and then to the crowds gathering on Milford village green.

The performance, a high point of the day's festivities, served to illustrate the close links between the men and ships of the Royal Navy – between Nelson and *Pickle* and Cornwallis. ⚓

THE NAVAL STAINED GLASS WINDOW

Continued on from page 46

The Red Ensign proved to be the biggest challenge, as the red colour changes when the glass is in the firing process and can either look too dark or become too light, thus appearing more on the orange spectrum. With each firing in the kiln using temperatures of up to 820 degrees Centigrade, the glass took a minimum of 24 hours to cool down. The whole process of the window's construction took a couple of months to complete.

Finally, there was the removal of the previous window in which great care had to be taken not to damage it. It is not always apparent how the original window had been fitted, as some are set into a rebate whilst others slot in to the stone. In this case it was set in a rebate so once removed, the stone work was cleaned and the new window fitted and fixed using a traditional lime mortar mix.

Hopefully the new window will join the rest of the church adornments and be viewed by successive generations of villagers and visitors alike. However, no doubt many questions will be asked why the ensign is coloured red when today's Royal Navy Flag is the white ensign. But Cornwallis and Man were Admirals of the Red at the time of their decease, and John Peyton was a Rear Admiral of the Red. The two lines of verse are from the *Elegy to the Admirals of Milford*. ⚓

HONOURING CORNWALLIS
by Barry Jolly

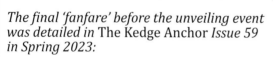

The final 'fanfare' before the unveiling event was detailed in The Kedge Anchor *Issue 59 in Spring 2023:*

The dedication of a memorial tablet in St Ann's Church, Portsmouth to Admiral Hon Sir William Cornwallis in June 2023 will be the culmination of a long campaign by The 1805 Club and Milford-on-Sea Historical Record Society for a national symbol of recognition for the services of a great admiral. That said, it was the essential modesty of Cornwallis that resulted in the lack of formal recognition. How, then, did this situation arise, and what were the implications?

In October 1793, twenty-five years before his death, and whilst he was serving as Commander-in-Chief East Indies, Cornwallis made a will in which he wrote, 'I desire that my Body if I die at sea may be wound up in an old cot or canvas, and thrown from the gangway into the sea in the same manner as the seamen are buried.' His personal effects were to be left to his flag captain, John Whitby.

A later, and final, will in 1816 did not specify the mode of burial, but 'He gave directions as to his funeral that he was to be buried "alongside his friend Captain John Whitby in Milford Churchyard", also that no tombstone or any kind of memorial was to be erected in his memory'. Cornwallis, evidently, had no desire for any form of ostentation or show.

The allusions to Whitby are illuminating. Whitby had gone out to India as a Midshipman, but had advanced to Post Captain at the age of just 18 through Cornwallis' patronage. On his death in 1806, Cornwallis took charge, smoothing the anxieties of Whitby's father, Rev Thomas Whitby, and commissioning a locket from the Cornish enameller, Henry Bone, for Mrs Whitby; the locket is now in the Gilbert Collection at the Victoria and Albert Museum. Mrs Whitby had been living at Cornwallis' home in Milford whilst her husband was at sea. On his death she moved away, but returned, with her sister Juliana Symonds as chaperone, at the earnest request of Cornwallis, as companion and carer, but very much in a quasi-father and daughter relationship as their correspondence, both earlier and subsequently, makes clear.

Neither of the two stipulations for Cornwallis' burial, recorded by Whitby's great grandson, George Cornwallis-West in his *The Life and Letters of Admiral Cornwallis*, can be verified, but the actual arrangements were

sufficiently intriguing for John Bewley, a member of The 1805 Club, to ask in 2013, about the whereabouts of the grave. The only clues were that it was at the west end of the church and next to that of Admiral Robert Man, now inconveniently covered in a passageway between the body of the church and the vestry. It was found by chance by MoSHRS member Ann Braid, based on some knowledge of relative location, a hunch, and being in the right place and time as the sun's rays fell on the grave at the right angle for reading the faded inscription. The broken gravestone was engraved on the top half only, recording the death of John Whitby. The grave has since been restored, and its re-dedication was reported in a special feature in the Autumn 2019 edition (No 52) of *The Kedge Anchor*.

The empty space in the lower half of the gravestone is curious, not least because four other people are interred there:

Cornwallis, Whitby's wife, Theresa, and their daughter, also Theresa (later Mrs West). The fourth is Mrs West's daughter, another Theresa who died unmarried in 1920. The difficulty, though, is apparent. The grave was intended for John and Theresa Whitby, and it would have been inappropriate for Cornwallis' name to be inscribed whether he wished it or not. Equally, there would have been some misgivings about adding Mrs Whitby to the inscription when the unmarked section of the gravestone was itself an unspoken memorial to Cornwallis. Mrs West resolved the dilemma by erecting a magnificent memorial in the church to all three – Cornwallis, Captain Whitby and Mrs Whitby – and a pendant recording the death of Mrs West was placed below this by her daughter when she joined the trio in 1886.

Later, there was one other personal tribute to Cornwallis, included in a volume of poems written by Mrs West and published in 1855. It is to be found in *The Sedan Chair; or, Fireside Memories,* an autobiographical poem of some 51 stanzas, each of nine lines, but, of which, none mention Cornwallis, or, indeed, anyone else, by name. Reviewers of the time were puzzled by the various allusions to unnamed people, and the poem was deciphered only recently. It can now be seen as a very personal tribute indeed: Cornwallis was Mrs West's godfather, was very much a quasi-paternal influence on her, and made her and Mrs Whitby the principal beneficiaries of his estate. The lines of verse inscribed on the memorial in St Ann's Church have been taken from this poem.

A memory of Mrs West illustrates

Cornwallis' attitude to honours. Whilst she was reading a book on peers of the realm, Cornwallis is reported to have said, 'Put that nonsense away. Don't you realise that half the men in that book are living on the reflected glory of their forebears? Why learn about them?... Honours are all very well in their way, but remember this, "Worth makes the man and want of it the fellow."'

These words attributed to Cornwallis, whether accurate for not, are nonetheless a faithful reflection of his attitude to honours. Indeed, he had been offered the Bath in 1795 following an action against more than overwhelming odds, known since as Cornwallis's Retreat.

The occasion was an encounter on 16-17 June 1795 when his squadron of five ships of the line and two frigates came up against the entire French Atlantic fleet out of Brest comprising no fewer than twelve French ships of the line and eighteen smaller vessels. He had, perhaps, been a little over ambitious in seeking to replicate the successful capture of several French ships a few days earlier, a success resented by Vice-Admiral Louis Thomas Villaret de Joyeuse, who put to sea in the hope of avenging the loss.

One ship, *Mars* (74), was sailing badly, an unfortunate and unwelcome echo of the situation in two earlier actions when Cornwallis faced larger French squadrons, under La Motte Piquet and de Ternay in March and June 1780 respectively. Rather than abandon even one ship, Cornwallis stood his own flagship between *Mars* and the French fleet. 'The foremost in the fight!', a phrase in the four lines of verse now inscribed on the new memorial in St Ann's Church, encapsulate this supreme example of courage and leadership.

At the height of the action, and in a classic *ruse de guerre*, Cornwallis detached one of his frigates, *Phaeton* (Captain Robert Stopford), which then sent signals to non-existent support over the horizon, and the French accordingly withdrew. The squadron suffered a mere 14 men wounded and none killed, a far lower number than the French.

It was Stopford who landed at Plymouth with the despatches, declaring, 'English Gallantry never more conspicuous than at such a moment, when we were apparently to be oppressed by numbers. Admiral Cornwallis has shewn himself equal to any undertaking.' His heartfelt qualification to this, '... though I hope no British ships will ever be in future so much risked,' is understandable.

The meritorious nature of the occasion was recognised instantly, and the reaction from ministers and friends alike was universally laudatory. Amongst the tributes, the First Sea Lord, Sir Charles Middleton, wrote to say that he had labelled Cornwallis's journal, 'Vice-Admiral Cornwallis's Retreat,' presumably the origin of the designation. Later in the year, both Houses of Parliament afforded him fulsome Votes of Thanks.

More immediately, the First Lord of the Admiralty, Earl Spencer, sent his own congratulations, before writing later the same day conveying the wish of George III to nominate Cornwallis for the vacant Riband of the Order of the Bath. The offer was declined, and declined again when the matter was pressed. Cornwallis also asked for the offer not to be made public, writing, 'I must again Humbly solicit permission to decline accepting it – and I shall endeavour to suppress my Vanity by not making it known that such a distinguished mark of

His Majesty's favour was intended.'

Others have echoed these encomiums down the years. Edward Pelham Brenton, who had served under Cornwallis in India, wrote that Cornwallis's Retreat is 'justly considered one of the finest displays of united courage and coolness to be found in our naval history.'

An undated lengthy poem of a rather different genre from that of Mrs West, paid fulsome tribute:

Aye, Blue Billy:—here's to him, with three
          times three,
To the honour of his name upon the sea!
'He upheld Old England's credit,'
said the country in its pride:
'Cornwallis's Retreat,'
Greek Xenophon's great feat,
In its spirit we may claim to set beside.

Various paintings were made, with the best known being that of Thomas Luny in 1834. Later still, in 1849, a medal was struck, the Citation stating, 'Brilliant repulse of a fleet four times superior in force.'

That this defensive action should have stood so long in the memory is remarkable, a fact recognised by Cuthbert Collingwood who wrote, 'It is extraordinary that Cornwallis, than whom no man stands higher for bravery and good conduct in action, should have established his character more by his retreats than by his victories.' [*See The Earlier Retreats in text box*]

Therein lies part of the problem. Cornwallis took part in fleet actions with distinction, notably at The Saintes in 1782, but never commanded a fleet in battle. It was a deficiency remarked on by his friend, Horatio Nelson:

'What a dreadful winter you have had my

Dear friend we must not compare our Medn weather with that of the Channel That you may very soon see the French outside of Brest is the fervent wish of
     Your Most Obliged & Sincere Friend
        Nelson & Bronte'

The Blockade of Brest in 1801 and from 1803 to 1806, to which Nelson alluded, was Cornwallis' crucial contribution to the frustration of Napoleon Bonaparte's plans for invasion of England and the defeat of the Franco-Spanish fleet at Trafalgar. Whatever the true intentions of Bonaparte, a matter of considerable conjecture and debate ever since, the threat was thought real enough at the time. Equally, the decisions made by Cornwallis in the weeks before Trafalgar were vital to that great victory.

Cornwallis held two sinecures, as a Vice-Admiral of The United Kingdom (appointed 1814) and as a Colonel of Marines (appointed 1787), which brought in a useful additional income. When still a Rear Admiral of Great Britain in 1800 (appointed 1796), his annual income from this source alone was £342/8/0d - about £37,000 in today's values. He was also made GCB in 1815 on the restructuring of that Order as part of a general recognition of the services of naval and military personnel at the end of the Napoleonic War. His position in the list, as the most senior untitled admiral, is telling.

Nonetheless, a national symbol of recognition and re-membrance of a great admiral is long overdue. His merits are now being given an official *imprimatur* by the memorial in St Ann's Church, to reflect the conviction of his good friend, Nelson, in a letter to the Duke of Clarence in 1804: 'Cornwallis I dare say merits everything a grateful Country can bestow for keeping the Enemy in Brest by a close blockade.'

These words from Nelson, for all his fame, success and, indeed, vanity, reflected a sincere and long-standing admiration and respect for Cornwallis, which was perhaps even more marked in a letter written sixteen years before when Nelson was on half pay without immediate prospects of employment:

'I always shall as I have ever done be ready to step forth whenever Service requires or My Friends may wish Me to serve. Fame says you are going out with a command [As Commodore, East Indies]. If in either Actual Service or a Wish of Yours to accept of one under Your Command who Reveres and Esteems You, I am willing and ready to go forth and by a Strict adherence to your orders as My Superior and Wishes as my Friend prove myself worthy of the friendship you have Honor'd me with, for indeed I am with great truth

Your Sincere and Affectionate
Horatio Nelson'

Nelson's respect, indeed the reverence

and esteem to which he refers, underlines Cornwallis' place in the pantheon of British admirals as no other could. The full stanza from Mrs West's poem delivers a definitive endorsement:

The nobly-born! the foremost in the fight!
Who 'mid the ocean's roar his power display'd,
True son of Britain! With the arm of might
He dared the foe in triple strength arrayed,
Their lilies shatter'd, and their hearts dismayed,
And singly upheld Britannia's walls of wood! –
He was God's noblest work – a man upright,
By grovelling minds but little understood;
Benevolent as brave, most just, most *true*
most good!

The Earlier Retreats

20-22 March 1780: Cornwallis' squadron of one 64, one 50 and one 44 met up with a larger French squadron under La Motte Piquet of two 74s, one 64, one 50 (mistaken for a second 64) and one 36. The 44 gun HMS *Janus* lost her mizzen topmast and fore topgallant mast, and had to be rowed away by boats set down byHMSs *Lion* and *Bristol*. The rear-guard action continued until fresh sail was sighted, and Cornwallis gave chase in the mistaken belief that more ships of the line were at hand. The belief was shared, and the French force bore away.

20 June 1780: With a larger squadron of two 74s, two 64s, one 50 and one 32, Cornwallis fell in with another superior French force under de Ternay, comprising one 80, two 74s, four 64s, three frigates and two corvettes. With HMS *Ruby* misplaced at a distance, skilful seamanship and courage were called for. De Ternay, though, believing that his convoy of troops under General Rochambeau bound for North America, declined significant action. Cornwallis' modesty on this occasion was in part necessary: '*les vaisseaux anglais s'échappèrent et s'en tirèrent plus glorieusement que nous.*'['the English ships escaped and fared more gloriously than we did'], wrote the Duc de Lauzon in his memoirs.

MEMORIAL UNVEILED TO ADMIRAL CORNWALLIS

The above headline appeared in Milford-on-Sea News and What's On, *and was followed by this article:*

Admiral the Hon Sir William Cornwallis (1744-1819) settled and lived at Newlands Manor, Milford-on-Sea from 1800. He was one of England's most renowned admirals, a friend of Lord Nelson, and with a long and distinguished Royal Navy career he is particularly remembered for frustrating Napoleon's plans to invade England.

In October 2013, the Milford-on-Sea Historical Record Society and the 1805 Club, embarked on a mission to find Admiral Cornwallis's grave, and this led to the 'Cornwallis Remembered' project and celebrations.

After much work to commemorate one of Milford-on-Sea's famous sons, 'Cornwallis Remembered' culminated last week, when a memorial was laid as permanent tribute to Admiral Cornwallis at St Ann's Church in Portsmouth Dockyard.

Those in attendance included Chris Hobby, chairman of the Cornwallis Remembered project, and historian, Barry Jolly of the Milford-on-Sea Historical Record Society (MoSHRS).

About 'Cornwallis Remembered'

The 'Cornwallis Remembered' project had started in October 2013, when The 1805 Club

contacted Milford-on-Sea Historical Record Society (MoSHRS) as they understood that Admiral Cornwallis was buried in Milford churchyard but "the grave had been lost".

However, according to his biographer George Cornwallis West, the Admiral had left instructions that he was to be 'buried at Milford near Captain Whitby' also that no tombstone or any kind of memorial was to be erected in his memory.

This last injunction Mrs Whitby obeyed to the letter.

However, Mrs Whitby's daughter, Theresa West, later erected a memorial in the church to the Admiral and her parents and the

inscription confirms that all three were "in the same vault at the western end of this churchyard".

All Saints Church, in Milford-on-Sea still has the memorial to Admiral Cornwallis, Captain John Whitby and Mrs M A T Whitby which was erected by Mrs West in 1852.

So to find the Admiral's grave it was necessary to find Captain Whitby's grave. The general area was known, although the grave was not immediately identifiable.

Early in 2014 one of the members of the Society chanced to look at the ledger on the grave outside the vestry door. Despite the wording being very worn, the low sun caught it at just the right angle and some of the wording could be made out. After researching safe methods of highlighting the inscription on the ledger, the first of which was inconclusive, the inscription was finally revealed.

The Admiral's grave had been found.

In May 2014 it was proposed that MoSHRS together with The 1805 Club, and with church agreement, should erect some form of identification for the Admiral's grave. MoSHRS members were informed in Spring 2015 about a proposal to conserve the Cornwallis/Whitby grave ledger and repair the memorial to Rear Admiral John Peyton who served at the same time as Cornwallis; re-siting the memorial when it was returned from repair. Faculty approval from the church had been received in

autumn 2016 and permission to proceed was received in March 2017. Donations were sought and received to complete this work.

Further research into the careers of Cornwallis and Whitby caused the Society to realise that there was a very important story to be told about the achievements of Admiral Cornwallis. This in turn led to the determination to prepare a commemoration of Cornwallis on the 200th anniversary of his death – and so "Cornwallis Remembered 1819-2019" was born.

In July 2019, hundreds of villagers and invited dignitaries enjoyed the Cornwallis Remembered celebrations which took place across Milford-on-Sea to mark the 200th anniversary of the admiral's passing.

Prior to the village celebrations a Cornwallis stained glass window was installed in All Saints' Church on Wednesday 5th June 2019.

The stained glass window was paid for by an anonymous donor and Milford-on-Sea Historical Record Society were involved in the design and wording of the details on the glass.

The window was by crafted and installed by Steve Sherriff, Stained Glass Specialist. It is now sits gloriously commemorating the Three Admirals and Captain John Whitby.

On Friday 5th July 2019, All Saints' Church, Milford-on-Sea held a service conducted by the Bishop of Basingstoke

VILLAGE GREEN EVENT FOR ALL THE FAMILY

Come and discover the story of Admiral Cornwallis and his Milford-on-Sea connections

See the two horse post-chaise with riders in full costume (arrives around 3.30pm). Plus, a variety of themed entertainment, live music, Royal Navy and Trafalgar Way stands.

Primary School presentation on the Wooden World Educational Workshop

Refreshments available locally.

EVERYONE WELCOME!

CORNWALLIS REMEMBERED 1819 – 2019

Friday 5th July 3pm to 5pm on the Village Green

with Senior representatives from Hampshire, the Royal Navy, the 1805 Club and Milford-on-Sea Historical Record Society attending.

There was also a rededication to the newly rediscovered Cornwallis grave and Peyton memorial.

The same day, a village Celebration of the Cornwallis Story was held on the village green with a host of attractions and activities, including the two horse post-chaise with riders in full costume.

Christopher Beeton (Senior village resident) & Post Chaise

The 'News of Trafalgar by Post-Chaise' visited the village school and then proceeded to the church service which was followed by a recreation of the arrival of the news of Nelson's death and victory at Trafalgar by post-chaise.

The two horse post-chaise then moved to the village green where there was a variety of live music, the Total Voice Chamber Choir performed, a Royal Navy marching display, Royal Navy and Trafalgar Way stands and refreshments provided by local village groups including the Primary School and Royal Navy Catering.

Also, as part of the Cornwallis

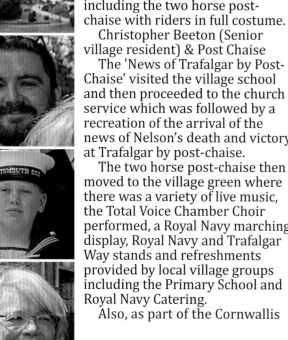

Remembered celebrations there was a Commemorative Dinner held on Saturday 6th July 2019 in the Cornwallis Suite of South Lawn Hotel, Milford-on-Sea with a leading naval historian as the guest speaker.

There was a Command of the Seas! Exhibition at St Barbe Museum and Art Gallery, Lymington.

Milford-on-Sea Historical Record Society published a commemorative Bicentenary Edition of its Occasional Magazine with articles on Cornwallis, Man and Peyton.

A Royal Navy training boat of the P2000 Archer Class attended Lymington port on the 5th July.

And there was a Wooden World educational workshops run by The 1805 Club at Milford-on-Sea Primary School. ☻

THE ADMIRALS' HERITAGE TRAIL

As a lasting resource, a heritage trail has been established from Hurst castle, through Milfod-on-Sea and surrounding towns and villages, and on to Buckler's Hard and Calshot Castle.

The sponsored leaflet comprises a comp-rehensive A2-sized fold-out map featuring the 24 highlights of the trail. All the illustrations on the leaflet are by local Milford-on-Sea artist Shaun Stevens and copies of the free leaflet are available from Milford-on-Sea newsagents, Hurst Castle shop or the Parish Council office [the latter kindly sent a copy to the Editor, from which the images on this page and on page 86 are reproduced].

A QR code for further information is given on page 86. ☻

COMMAND OF THE SEAS
THE NAVY AND THE NEW FOREST AGAINST NAPOLEON
by Barry Jolly

Early in the planning for the whole Cornwallis Remembered programme, consideration was given to an exhibition to be held at St Barbe Museum and Art Gallery in nearby Lymington. Difficulties were at once placed in the way. Would an exhibition be a viable proposition? How easy would it be, if at all, to convince the residents of Lymington to visit? How could we possibly envisage a naval exhibition unless it was centred on Nelson? How much would it cost, and could we raise the necessary funding?

Perhaps worst of all, and a question underlying the entire programme, how could we possibly laud our three admirals – Cornwallis, Robert Man and John Peyton – when the reputation of two of these lay in tatters?

Clearly, the last of these difficulties had to be tackled, and fast.

Rear Admiral John Peyton has attracted little interest among naval historians over the years. Peyton had been in command of HMS *Defence* (74) at the Battle of Aboukir Bay in 1798, and, as such, was one of Nelson's Band of Brothers, but the Oxford Dictionary of Naval Biography damned him with faint praise; others have followed with equal lack of care.

John Peyton was the grandson of an admiral, and the son of a naval civil servant. This may explain how a man of modest abilities reached captain's rank. He suffered from ill health, and was anxious to go home, but he commanded his ship with good sense and courage. [Oxford DNB]

Extraordinary as it may seem from such a source, the description (and even date of birth) was quite inaccurate. Peyton's father was an admiral and his grandfather a commodore, both of whom served to good effect. There was, it must be admitted, a brother whose promotion to flag rank was blocked after a less than illustrious career and a high degree of hanky-panky with the wife of another officer, but John Peyton himself, though no high flier, was a sound captain who distinguished himself at the Battle of Aboukir Bay in 1798, taking the surrender of the French *Franklin*.

To correct this state of affairs, an article was published in *The Trafalgar Chronicle* (2019) with a scathing critique of past injustices and a staunch defence of Peyton himself. One omission, though, was a letter from Nelson himself a few months after the battle:

> It never was much in my power to shew you those attentions which in every way your conduct entitled you to. ... I beg you will make my best Compt: to your Brother of the Navy Office and Believe me with every sentiment of Regard your obliged & affectionate Friend. Nelson.

This was scarcely the letter of an admiral dissatisfied with the conduct of one of his captains; nor was Nelson so dismissive of the merits of Peyton's

brother (rather than father) at the Navy Board.

Admiral Robert Man posed an equal, if not greater, challenge. Ever since Clowes' naval history of 1897, Man has been accused of dereliction of duty, with Clowes' withering judgement - when Man's squadron reached home, his action "was severely disapproved, and he was ordered to strike his flag, nor was he again employed afloat" accepted as gospel.

An admiral being ordered to strike his flag is routine whatever the circumstances, and Man did serve again ... as a Lord Commissioner of the Admiralty, scarcely a role for someone guilty of neglect of duty. An article in *The Mariner's Mirror* in 2018 – 'A Good Man in Every Sense of the Word – The Reputation of Robert Man' – provided a considered examination of all the relevant facts, rather than simply accepting Jervis' need for a scapegoat after he was forced to yield the Mediterranean in 1797, and led to an entirely different conclusion.

The standing of Admiral Cornwallis has never been in doubt, and yet the reasons for his status as one of Britain's leading admirals bears repeating. Cornwallis was a leading captain in many engagements, not least at the battle of the Saintes in 1782, and more than once demonstrated remarkable skill and courage in extricating himself from testing situations. Most of all, his conduct of the Blockade of Brest before and after the peace of Amiens merited, as his good friend Nelson observed, 'everything which a grateful country can bestow...'

The focus of the projected exhibition was on these three admirals and, by association with Cornwallis, Captain John Whitby and Mrs M A T Whitby. To be successful, sufficient material artefacts relating to these was essential. Fortunately, the article on John Peyton brought pride and relief to his descendants, and the ready release of portraits, believed to be by Dance, for display. The Whitby portraits are in the possession of the Strickland family of Sizergh Castle in Westmoreland, and past research articles on the Strickland family over an extended period paved the way to the loan of these key portraits.

We were fortunate that the Locket (*qv*) created for Mrs Whitby by Admiral Cornwallis was in a collection at the Victoria and Albert Museum which had been withdrawn from display as part of a refurbishment programme. We were less lucky with the cost: a bullet proof glass case fitted by the V&A's own staff necessarily accounted for a tidy sum.

Fortune did not smile on us wholly when it came to the portrait of Robert Man by Francis Rigaud at the NMM. The loan fee was hefty enough, but we would also have to pay a very stiff sum for essential repairs. In the event we settled for a copy which, when printed on vellum, certainly looked the part. The NMM came up trumps, however, with two ship models: would *Guadeloupe* (28) and *Minerva* (38) be of any use? Would they ever! *Guadeloupe* was Cornwallis' first command, and *Minerva* was the first command of his protege, John Whitby.

Other items of interest were Samuel Hood's uniform (as Captain), a sketch by Turner and an oil painting of the Battle of the Nile by Philip de Loutherbourg, a collection of naval medals of the time belonging to a member of The 1805 Club,

and The Nore Drum, a treasured possession of Lymington and Pennington Town Council believed to have been used during the escape from the clutches of The Nore mutineers in 1797 by a local hero, Admiral Sir Harry Neale.

The perceived need in some quarters for Nelson's name to be used in the exhibition title was resisted fiercely in Milford; our view was that the exhibition should concentrate on our three admirals without dilution. Eventually, we turned the problem round by pitting our locality against the Corsican Ogre: hence 'The Navy and the New Forest Against Napoleon'. The significance of the New Forest in providing timber for ships will not be lost on readers. We were assisted greatly by James Brown of the New Forest National Parks Authority, whose knowledge and expertise proved to be invaluable. The third of the three galleries at St Barbe was given over to this aspect of the exhibition, as may be seen in the accompanying photograph.

The challenging task of raising ever increasing sums of money was undertaken successfully by Chris Sanders of MoSHRS. Rosalyn Goulding, Collections

and Engagement Officer at St Barbe, applied her extensive experience to the equally challenging task of planning and design. Eventually the doors were opened, and some 3700 people attended the exhibition over the ensuing for twelve weeks.. From a personal perspective, it was gratifying to see so many historic artefacts on display in their natural milieu.

Just as important was the reaction of visitors; feedback questionnaires were uniformly eulogistic as the two following examples attest:

"One of the very best exhibitions I've been to in the past 10 years. British History is fascinating, and our naval/military exploits are second to none – interestingly Cornwallis is as great a naval leader as Nelson (but not sadly as famous)."

"Amazed at the high standard of presentation as well as exhibits. Delighted to see the paintings in Lymington. The National Gallery would be pleased to have such an exhibition. Very impressive. Thanks also for the explanation by local volunteers."

Joseph Mallord William Turner
Sketch for The Battle of Trafalgar

You are invited to the Private View of

Command of the Seas:
The Navy and the New Forest against Napoleon

THE SOURCE OF THE INSCRIPTION ON THE CORNWALLIS MEMORIAL WALL TABLET
by Barry Jolly

In February 1855, the personal columns of leading London newspapers advertised a book by Theresa C I West entitled, *Frescoes and Sketches from Memory*. The title obscured the contents of the book, which turned out to be a collection of poetry rather than drawings and paintings. Equally obscure was the identity of the author; embarrassed by her Christian names, she had altered her initials, and their order, rendering her own identity even less clear.

In fact, she was Theresa John Cornwallis West, the daughter of Captain John Whitby - the almost perennial flag captain of Admiral Cornwallis - and the god-daughter and heiress of Cornwallis himself.

Even with this knowledge, the anthology presented problems. A review in *The Atlas* was typical of the generally expressed opinions: The poems 'evidently depict much of her personal life. Into this we have no desire to pry: she is a woman who has felt and suffered much.' The discretion of *The Atlas* was of little help to its readers, and the very first interpretation and decoding of the autobiographical verse was in a suitably obscurely titled article – 'Poetry or autobiography: The verses of a Victorian lady' – published in the MoSHRS *Occasional Magazine* in 2018.

The poetry is Romantic in style, reflecting the time of Mrs West's

early years rather than the more modern style of Browning and Tennyson. It is nonetheless of some quality, written in impeccable metre, soundly constructed, and revealing a remarkable gift for languages: some poems are in French, some in Italian, with one translated into Italian from the original Portuguese.

One extended poem – of fifty one stanzas each of nine lines – is autobiographical in nature, but without identifying any of the people characterised in verse. Nonetheless, when deciphered, it reveals much about Mrs West's early life. John Whitby died when she was only a few months old. To Mrs West, born at Newlands, Cornwallis' home in Milford, Cornwallis became a quasi-paternal figure and a major influence on her life: 'My more than father! benefactor! friend!' Cornwallis helped Mrs Whitby over her bereavement:

Thine ears are open to the widow's prayer;
The orphans' [sic] cries are never raised in vain;

And provided

…. her refuge; and thy good-ness gave
A happy home – a kind protector's care

Problems arose with John Whitby's family, his father, Revd Thomas Whitby, laying claim to his fortune and later, a brother, George, refusing to repay a substantial loan:

Heartless kinsmen stung
My blood to venom. Thou alone couldst steep
The vow of vengeance, from just anger wrung.

In spite of this, Mrs West became a close friend of her aunt, Lucy Whitby, who married Edward Portman of Bryanston. When Mrs Whitby left Newlands after her husband's death, in accordance with the dictates of propriety, she returned at Cornwallis' request: 'Can you not bring yourself to solace the remaining years of an old man, who has ever looked on you as a daughter, and who has flattered himself that his affection and regard were in some measure returned?' (Quoted in G Cornwallis-West *Life and Letters of Admiral Cornwallis*.) Astonishingly, some suggestions of impropriety circulated:

Yet reputation shall pass on from challenge freed.
Banished from hence be foul Detraction's tongue,
Who lighting Error, is to Virtue blind!

Mrs West's early life, and character, are explored, and there are also some mixed messages about marriage. Of particular family note, however, are words addressed to the younger of the two sons who survived infancy. The older of the two had changed for the worse – insobriety and debt - after the innocent misfortune of killing a man in a carriage accident, and Mrs West then invested much hope in the younger, whose Christian names – William Cornwallis – themselves say much.

Child! Who that dear and honour'd name dost bear,
See that thou keep it spotless, void of stain.

Mrs West was to be disappointed in this; she regarded, with some considerable justification, her daughter-in-law as entirely unsuitable and the marriage caused a rupture which was never healed. So then to Cornwallis the naval officer. It was from Mrs West's autobiographical poem that the lines of verse inscribed on the memorial at St Ann's Church in Portsmouth naval base were taken. There was insufficient room for the full stanza to be inscribed on the memorial tablet, but it can be reproduced here in full:

The nobly-born! the foremost in the fight!
Who 'mid the ocean's roar his power display'd,
True son of Britain! With the arm of might
He dared the foe in triple strength arrayed,
Their lilies shatter'd, and their hearts dismayed,
And singly upheld Britannia's walls of wood!
He was God's noblest work – a man upright,
By grovelling minds but little understood;
Benevolent as brave, most just, most *true*,
most good!

CODA:
MEMORIAL TO ADMIRAL CORNWALLIS IN MILFORD CHURCH
By Barry Jolly

The memorial to Admiral Cornwallis in Milford Church [see pp 25, 61 & 66 and right] was erected by Theresa West. The memorial includes also Captain John Whitby and his wife Mary Anne Theresa together with an addendum to Theresa West, who was their daughter. There are factual errors in the text, as noted herein.

'**I**n a vault at the western end of this churchyard are deposited the remains of the Honourable Sir William Cornwallis G.C.B. Admiral of the Red Squadron of His Majesty's fleet, Rear Admiral of England[1] &c &c &c, son of James 5th Earl Cornwallis[2] and brother of the first Marquess, by Elizabeth, daughter of the Marquess of Townsend.[3] He was born February 20th 1744. As a naval Commander his services occupy a proud page in our national annals. He particularly distinguished himself in the command of the Canada under Sir George, afterwards Lord Rodney, April 12th 1782, in the West Indies. His celebrated retreat off Brest in which he withdrew his small squadron from an overpowering number of the enemy, on the 17th June 1795 was never equalled, and obtained for him the thanks of both Houses of Parliament. In 1806 he retired from the command of the Channel fleet to his seat, Newlands, in this parish, where he closed a well-spent life, after long suffering heroically borne, July 5th 1819, universally loved and respected. Practising every virtue, he was remarkable for truth, integrity, courage, benevolence, and unostentatious hospitality. In accordance with that modesty which was the distinguishing feature of his character, he left an expressed desire that no monument should be raised to his memory, which his successor Mrs Whitby, the widow of his friend and flag captain, deemed herself bound to obey, but this tribute to his virtues and the honour of her country, her daughter Mrs Frederick West feels it her duty to erect to the benefactor who cherished her infancy with parental solicitude, and whose memory she reveres with affection, gratitude, and admiration.

In the same vault with the ashes of his friend the Honourable Admiral Cornwallis who desired expressly to be buried beside

him, are interred those of Captain John Whitby RN eldest son of the Revd Thomas Whitby of Creswell Hall, in the County of Stafford. He entered the Navy at the early age of 12 years, and during a period of 20 years was constantly and actively engaged in the service of his profession. Into the Minerva frigate, then bearing the flag of his patron, and friend, Admiral Cornwallis, he was made Post in 1793. He was brave and handsome, his heart tender, generous, and sincere. Zealous in his profession, loyal to his Sovereign, and attached to his country, he yet found leisure for cultivating vast and varied powers of mind with assiduous care, so that few subjects eluded his grasp. But it pleased providence to cut short a life of so much public, and private promise, and this gallant officer sunk under a brief but severe illness soon after his appointment to the Ville de Paris, on the 6th April 1806,[4] at Newlands, in the County of Hants. Deeply and deservedly lamented.

In the same vault reposes the body of Mary Anne Theresa Whitby, daughter of the late Captain Thomas Symonds and of Elizabeth Malet his wife who was born December 18th AD 1784[5] and rendered up her soul to God August 5th 1850 suddenly, and painlessly, at Newlands in this parish. The affectionate and faithful wife of John Whitby Esq Post Captain Royal Navy, she possessed unfeigned piety, and masculine sense, with every feminine charm of person, the desire of being useful to her species, and cordiality towards numerous friends who lament her loss. Her intellect was penetrating, her accomplishments varied, she was the benefactress of the poor, and the stay of many. Her grateful and afflicted daughter raises this memorial to an excellent mother, tenderly wept, and affectionately beloved, trusting in the hope

of a blessed resurrection, and reunion in the kingdom of heaven.

Also to the memory of Theresa J Cornwallis West, of Newlands Manor in this parish, widow of Frederick R West of Ruthin Castle, North Wales, born May 1st 1804,[6] died September 18th 1886. My purposes are ended, and the thoughts of my heart: but my trust is in thee, my God and my Redeemer. Have mercy upon thy servant O Lord, and blot out all my transgressions.'

The memorial was commissioned by Mrs Theresa West, Cornwallis' god-daughter, and designed by John Henry Foley (1818-74). The decorative element – entitled 'Grief' – was exhibited at the Royal Academy in 1852 before installation. Foley's work includes Goldsmith and Burke for Trinity College Dublin, John Stuart Mill on the Thames Embankment, and Faraday, Reynolds and Barry for Westminster Palace Yard. A small addendum is dedicated to Mrs West, erected by her youngest daughter, also Theresa. 🕮

NOTES

There are errors in the text, in spite of the authors being Mrs Theresa West and her youngest daughter, also Theresa:

[1]   In fact he held the position of Vice Admiral of the United Kingdom (although often still referred to as of Great Britain) which was an honorary position. See The London Gazette of 14th May 1814 p 1007.

[2]   His father was fifth Baron Cornwallis rather than fifth Earl, but was created first Earl Cornwallis in 1753.

[3]   His mother was the daughter of the second Viscount Townshend – the 'h' is the correct spelling – who died in 1738. His grandson, the fourth Viscount, was created Marquess Townshend in 1787, but Cornwallis was not descended from the Marquess.

[4]   The date in the locket made by Cornwallis for Mrs Whitby is 7th April 1806. See Jolly, Barry *Mrs. Whitby's Locket - The story of England's youngest ever naval captain and his redoubtable wife* See p 28.

[5]   18th December 1783; see *Mrs. Whitby's Locket* p 28.

[6]   1st May 1805; see *Mrs. Whitby's Locket* p 28.

MILFORD-ON-SEA

1, 2 & 3
Graves of Admiral Cornwallis, Captain John Whitby and Theresa Whitby

4. All Saints' Church
5. Milford House

CULMINATION

Finally, in The 1805 Dispatches *of August 2023, the deed had been done and a brief report was given as below. This was decidedly brief because it was hoped at the time that this book would be produced, recording all that had happened hitherto and giving an opportunity to show many photographs of both the final event and from earlier events, for which there had not previously been space to publish them. They randomly follow this piece of text.*

As everyone who was able to attend will know, members of The 1805 Club and our colleagues from the Milford-on-Sea Historical Record Society had a wonderful day at HM Naval Base, Portsmouth, on Friday 16 June, 2023. The occasion was the laying of a memorial plaque commemorating Admiral Cornwallis. from the day are shown, with few details, because we are planning to prepare and issue a commemorative document recording the whole ten-year history leading up to and including this event. This will probably be issued digitally, with just a few printed copies for special participants to retain, because the distribution cost to all members far outweighs the cost of

printing (If a sponsor were to step up, this decision is negotiable).

In this edition of The 1805 Dispatches, just some small pictures

The day started with a very moving service in St Ann's Church [see page 8], which included a reading by our Chaplain, the Rev. Lynda Sebbage. After the service the congregation gathered outside for the unveiling of the plaque and a few group photos, including one of the Sea Cadet troop who looked after us in the dockyard, where we were not allowed to 'wander off'. We then repaired to the garden of Admiralty House, courtesy of the Second Sea Lord, for an enjoyable garden party, in blazing sun, where we were treated to a fine talk about Cornwallis by Professor Andrew Lambert [see page 10], who is considered the current expert on the admiral.

(See ensuing pages for a few more pix)
You may also enjoy looking at the Milford-on-Sea Blogspot, which you will find at: https://milfordonsea.blogspot.com/2023/06/ memorial-unveiled-to-admiral-cornwallis. html ⚓

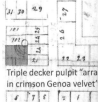

Triple decker pulpit "arra in crimson Genoa velvet'

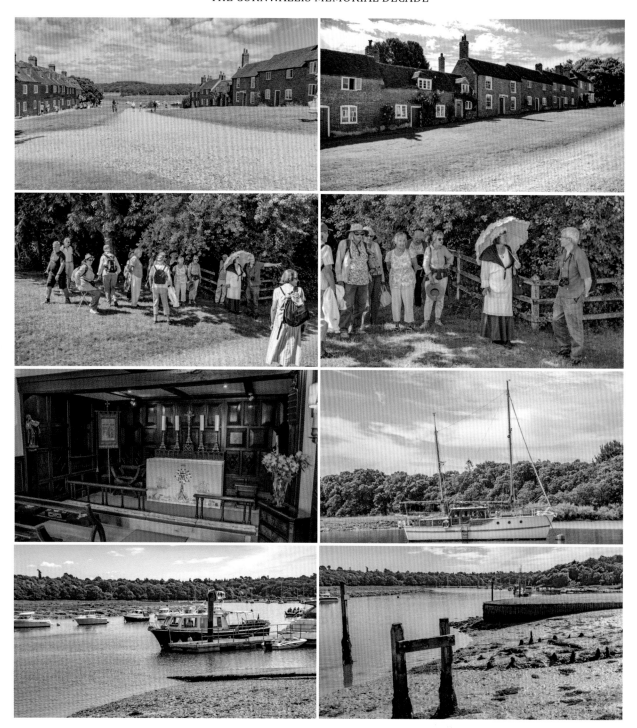

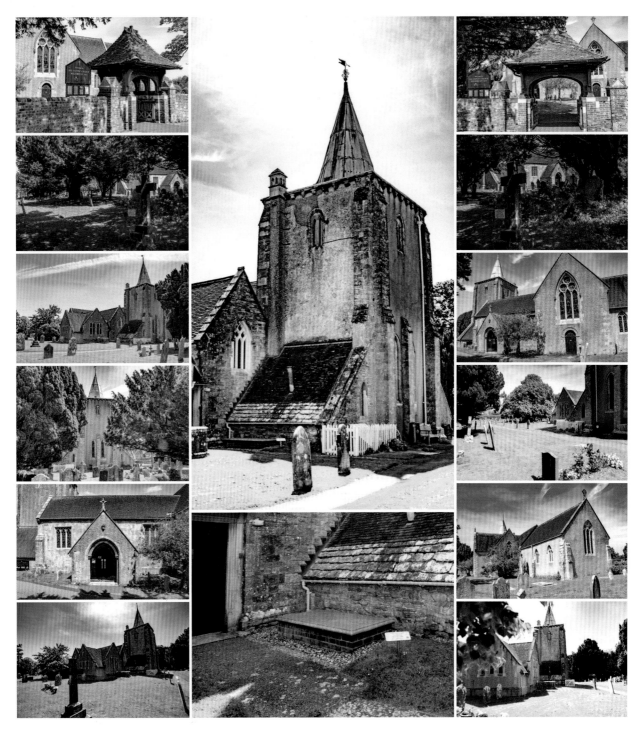

THE FUNERAL OF ADMIRAL CORNWALLIS
By Chris Sanders

The commemoration of Admiral **Cornwallis** triggered a great deal of research by members of Milford-on-Sea Historical Record Society (MoSHRS), much of which was published in the Society's research publication, the Occasional Magazine. Two articles from MoSHRS's Occasional Magazine Volumes 6 and 7 have been blended into a single abridged version here.

Late in 1816, at Salisbury, when returning from a driving excursion, Admiral Cornwallis had a stroke and, for the next three years, he was nursed at Newlands Manor by Mrs Whitby who managed his estates. In the spring of 1819, he contracted a chill.

Mrs Whitby was the widow of Cornwallis' close friend, Captain John Whitby RN. The Whitby's had a daughter who, in later years, kept a memoir which records "He sat for three days in an armchair in the library, mostly sleeping, and watched with the tenderest care by my mother and myself. On the afternoon of July 5th after a vain effort to try to get him to take his medicine, they thought to accomplish it through me. He replied,' Don't torment me!' then opening his eyes, he saw who it was; he took my hand (I was only thirteen at the time), and said: 'My dear! My dear! God bless you always.' He never spoke again and passed away with my hand still in his."

The newspapers of the time carried a short notice of his death, which was repeated either in full or in summary in national and local publications including 10th July "Morning Post" and "Morning Chronicle". Given the thrust and tenor of the words, the notice was probably written by Mrs Whitby herself:

DEATH OF ADMIRAL CORNWALLIS

On the 5th inst. died, at his seat at Newlands, in the county of Southampton, the Hon. Sir William Cornwallis, G.C.B. Vice-Admiral of England &c. The naval annals of this country are graced with the names of few individuals who stand so pre-eminent as that of the late Sir William Cornwallis. Silence on occasions of this nature (as to any panegyric of the deceased), may be deemed eloquence: in the present instance, the deep and unaffected regret of numerous friends for private worth – the gratitude of his country, for many and very distinguished public services, will add more to the posthumous splendour of such a character, than the sculptured urn or marble monument can, even with sufficient truth, hand down to succeeding generations.

The funeral was arranged for Friday 16th July and as the Milford Parish Register notes the ceremony was performed by the Reverend William Thompson, curate.

A report of the Admiral's funeral appeared in the Hampshire Telegraph and Sussex Chronicle, and General Advertiser for Hants, Sussex, Surrey, Dorset, and Wilts of 19 July 1819:

"LYMINGTON, July 16] On Friday morning were interred, at the Parish Church of Milford, the remains of the Hon. Admiral Sir William Cornwallis, G.C.B. The body was attended to the grave by all the members of his own household, and a few of his immediate friends and neighbours, as pall-bearers – Commissioner the Hon. Sir George Grey, Bart. was Chief Mourner, supported by his son, and Captain Ward, R.N. – Admiral Lord Northesk, G.C.B. Adm Sir H. Neale, Bart, Sir James W. Gardiner, Bart. Rev. Thomas Rivett, Rev. Geo. Burrard,

Capt. T. Symonds, R.N. Wm. Reynolds, Esq and Robert Budden, Esq. were all pall-bearers. The large concourse of all ranks of people whom this melancholy occasion drew together (among whom were forty Charity children, objects of the Admiral's bounty, dressed in mourning, and conducted by their Matrons), as well as the carriages of the principal families in the vicinity, may, in some faint degree, bear testimony to the great respect so generally felt for a character sustained through the whole course of a long life upon the soundest principles of true Christianity and unaltered integrity."

A brief explanation of those named in the report helps to appreciate their connections with Admiral Cornwallis:

- The chief mourner, Commissioner the Hon. Sir George Grey, Bart. 1st Baronet, KCB, was the son-in-law of Lady Mary Cornwallis, William's younger sister. He served in the Royal Navy on active service from 1781 to 1804. At the time of the funeral, he was Commissioner at Portsmouth Dockyard.
- George Grey, a great nephew to Cornwallis, 20 years old, inherited the baronetcy in 1828. He was to serve as Home Secretary in three separate Whig administrations.
- Captain Charles Warde, R.N., 33 years old, the grandson of Lady Charlotte Cornwallis, an older sister of William. Warde had served in HMS Glory, a 98-gun ship of the line, under his great uncle's flag and Cornwallis formed a good opinion of him.
- Admiral Lord Northesk, G.C.B. served under Cornwallis during the blockade of Brest. HMS Britannia carried his flag and he was directed by Cornwallis to join Calder off Ferol. He subsequently joined Collingwood off Cadiz and was third in command at Trafalgar.
- Admiral Sir Harry Neale, Bart. of Walhampton a local dignitary living in Lymington

- Sir James Whalley-Smythe-Gardiner, 3rd Baronet, local resident.
- Rev. Thomas Rivett, local resident and landowner.
- Rev. George Burrard, of Yarmouth and brother to Admiral Sir Harry Neale.
- Captain Thomas Edward Symonds R.N., later Admiral, brother of Mrs Whitby and local resident.
- Wm. Reynolds, Esq, Mrs Whitby's brother-in-law and local resident.
- Robert Budden, Magistrate, Cornwallis' Solicitor and local resident.

The Admiral was buried in a vault in the west end of the churchyard alongside his friend Captain Whitby.

Readers may wish to find out more about the location of the vault by reading "Admiral Cornwallis; the search for the grave" by Bob Braid on page 44 in this publication. ❂

HON. WILLIAM   CORNWALLIS
Admiral of the   Blue Squadron
Rear Admiral   of England

PICTURE CAPTIONS AND CREDITS

Given the extended time period and diversity of the events and photographs included in this book,
it has not proved possible to identify all the subjects in the pictures, nor the source of them all.
Those that have been identified are listed in this table. I apologise for any errors of identification.

Page	Caption	Credit
Front Cover	*Admiral Cornwallis* By Thomas Uwins	Royal Museums Greenwich
Frontispiece	Final Memorial Stone Design	South Coast Memorials
7	The Commemorative Stone	
8	St Ann's Church HMNB Portsmouth	
9	St Ann's Church HMNB Portsmouth	Paul French, Coolhat
10	Prof Andrew Lambert	
11	Prof Andrew Lambert and Fans	
14	Capt John Rodgaard & Chris Hobby	
19	John Bewley MBE and Juliet Bewley	Bob Braid MoSHRS
21	All Saints' Milford-on-Sea A Treasure-Trove of Naval History	
22	Members of the Milford-on-Sea Historical Record Society. Left to Right: Christopher Hobby (Vice Chairman), Dr Joanna Close Brooks, Bob Braid, Mrs Daphne Austin and Jim Butterworth.	These pictures are taken from the archives of the Milford-on-Sea Historical Record Society and supplied by Mr Jim Butterworth a member of the society's committee who has been digitising their records. Authorised by the churchwardens he recently carried out a computer documentation survey of the churchyard (4,300 deceased) and the church monuments 90+. The Club is grateful for his help and friendliness and also that of the Society. The image of Man by Rigaud is owned by the National Maritime Museum.
23	*Captain Robert Man 1779*, by John Francis Rigaud.	
23	There is no memorial to Admiral Man his plain gravestone is within the church.	
24	The copper plate indicating the grave of John Goodwin Gregory Peyton, Rear Admiral of the Red Squadron is situated in the centre aisle of the nave and states he died 2 August 1809 Aged 56 years.	
24	Rear Admiral John Peyton wall monument erected by his widow, unfortunately the detail in the lower inscription is illegible and unrecorded.	
25	Priestlands the former home of Admiral Peyton. He bought the house and its extensive grounds on his retirement as a Captain in 1800. It is now a local authority sixth form college.	
26	Captain John Whitby	
26	Mary Anne Theresa Whitby	Courtesy of Mrs Alice Loftie
27	Newlands Manor in 1832 the house and grounds would have been the same at the time of Theresa Whitby and Admiral Cornwallis.	From R A Grove "Views of Lymington' (1832)
28	Newlands Manor remains today in private hands as separate accommodations.	Keith Evans, The 1805 Club
29	Top: Newlands.	Keith Evans, The 1805 Club
29	The only memorial to this great sailor and Englishman remains today in All Saints, Milford-on-Sea.	Keith Evans, The 1805 Club
32	The Grave, unrestored	Bob Braid, MoSHRS
33	Two Important MoSHRS Publications: MoSHRS *Occasional Magazine* for 2019	Cover Image from Barry Jolly
34	Captain John Whitby on Mrs Whitby's locket itself	From the cover of B Jolly 'Mrs Whitby's Locket' (original photographs from the Victoria and Albert Museum.)
35	Left to Right, Front row: Jim Butterworth Secretary MoSHRS, Brian Giles Chairman, MoSHRS. Back row: Chris Hobby and Bob Braid.	Bob Braid MoSHRS
35	*Admiral The Honourable Sir William Cornwallis GCB* after Daniel Gardner 1775.	Naval Chronicle 1802
36	Detail of the Whitby/Cornwallis grave. The stone was most probably broken when it was moved from its original site within the churchyard.	Bob Braid MoSHRS
36	*Captain Robert Man, 1779* by John Francis Rigaud.	National Maritime Museum
37	The monument to Admiral John Goodwin Gregory Peyton within All Saints Church.	Bob Braid MoSHRS
37	Admiral Robert Man's gravestone is surprising for its simplistic inscription which covers less than a quarter of the stone including the spelling of his name.	Bob Braid MoSHRS
38	Stephen Tregidgo	Bob Braid MoSHRS
39	All Saints Church Milford-on-Sea	Bob Braid MoSHRS
40	South Lawn Hotel Milford-on-Sea	Not Known
42	The restored grave at All Saint's Church, Milford-on-Sea.	Bob Braid MoSHRS
42	The information plaque installed at the grave.	Bob Braid MoSHRS
44	Left: Memorial to Cornwallis in All Saint's Church. Right: The Grave, unrestored	Bob Braid MoSHRS
45	Left Top: The restored grave. Left Bottom: The information plaque installed at the grave.	Bob Braid MoSHRS
45	Right: Location of the grave pre-1933.	Not Known
46	Top: Three Admirals' Window; Centre: Nathan Sherriff installing; Bottom Left: Nathan Sherriff, Right Steve Sherriff.	Bob Braid MoSHRS
47	Various images of the replica of HMS *Pickle*	Paul French, Coolhat
49	Buckler's Hard	bucklershard.co.uk
51	Nigel Atkinson Esq. HM Lord-Lieutenant of Hampshire lays a wreath on the grave of Admiral Sir William Cornwallis GCB.	Bob Braid MoSHRS
52	Left to Right: Revd Lynda Sebbage, The 1805 Club, and Revd Dominic Furness, St Mary's, The Rt Revd David Williams , Bishop of Basingstoke, The Rt Revd Debbie Sellin, the Bishop of Southampton hidden, Revd Bernard Clarke RNR welcome The Lord Lieutenant. On duty is the Lord Lieutenant's Cadet. Rebecca Lee (police cadet).	Bob Braid MoSHRS
53	Top Left: Then *KA* Editor and Vice President Kenneth Flemming with Vice President Keith Evans, The 1805 Club, arrive at All Saint's Church, Milford.	Bob Braid MoSHRS
53	Top Right: John Bewley MBE and Juliet Bewley, The 1805 Club, arrive for the celebrations.	Bob Braid MoSHRS
53	Bottom: Lt Cdr Michael Cornwallis (RN Ret) and son Richard Cornwallis (left and slightly behind) came from Australia for the event. They are descended from Cornwallis' brother, James Cornwallis, 3rd Earl Cornwallis and Bishop of Lichfield. Next is Peter Mills descended from Charlotte, one of the Admiral's sisters. The lady is Julia Wykeham Martin also descended from James, the Bishop.	Bob Braid MoSHRS
54	Top: Milford Primary School Choir.	Bob Braid MoSHRS
54	Bottom: Dr James Soper member of Lymington Choral Society talking with the lady members of the church who checked in the guests and directed them to their seats.	Bob Braid MoSHRS

Page	Caption	Credit
55	A contingent of young sailors and officers in their first weeks of training from HMS *Collingwood* at Fareham, Hants, and HMS *Sultan* at Gosport, Portsmouth, await entry into St Mary's for the Commemoration Service.	Bob Braid MoSHRS
55	Bottom: The Parade was led by a fine Band of Sea Cadets from the Poole Division.	
57	'Sunset' was sounded by Bugler Bandsman Mike Thomas, Band of HM Royal Marines, Portsmouth, at the laying of the wreath followed by the 'Alert'. Richard and Lt Cdr Michael Cornwallis (RN Ret) are on the left.	
58	Top: *Admiral The Honourable Sir William Cornwallis GCB* after Daniel Gardner 1775.	National Maritime Museum
58	Bottom: *Captain Robert Man, 1779* by John Francis Rigaud.	National Maritime Museum
59	John Peyton.	From the portrait by Dance in the ownership of Kester Armstrong. Copyright with K Armstrong.
59	Rear Admiral John Peyton Memorial.	Bob Braid MoSHRS
60	Left: The Three Admirals Window in All Saints Church, Milford, in situ.	Bob Braid MoSHRS
60	Right: The The Three Admirals Window detail.	
61	Various pictures of the celebrations on Milford-on-Sea village green.	
62	Ditto.	
63	Top: Ditto.	
63	Bottom: AB&OS joining in the fun.	Galf (Peter Turner)
64	Newlands Manor and Parkland.	Keith Evans, The 1805 Club
64	Newlands estate including lake and farm lands, Milford-on-Sea and the Solent. Drone Picture.	Simon and Amy Davies Milford-on-Sea.
65	The Right Honourable Earl Howe GBE	Not Known
65	Sir Jonathon Band GCB DL	Not Known
66	Left HMS *Trumpeter*; Right: HMS *Pickle*	Bob Braid MoSHRS
68	*William Cornwallis as Admiral* by Daniel Gardner (1750-1805) Engraver William Ridley.	NMM PAD3292
68	All Saint's Church, Milford-on-Sea.	Paul French, Coolhat
69	The plaque installed with the grave at All Saint's Church.	Bob Braid MoSHRS
69	Memorial to Cornwallis in All Saint's Church	Paul French, Coolhat
70	*Cornwallis's Retreat, June 17, 1795* by Thomas Luny	Public domain
74	Top: Memorial to Cornwallis in All Saint's Church	Keith Evans, The 1805 Club
74	Bottom: 'Cornwallis Remembered' logo	Milford-on-Sea News & What's On
75	Detail of the Memorial Window.	Bob Braid MoSHRS
76	Advertisement for the Events	Milford-on-Sea News & What's On
76	Christopher Beeton (Senior Resident) meeting Lt Lapenotiere (actor Rob Hinwood)	Bob Braid MoSHRS
77	The restored grave.	
77	The plaque installed with the grave.	
77	Sponsors of The Admirals' Heritage Trail.	Photo by Peter Turner
79-81	Various images of St Barbe's Museum	Bob Braid MoSHRS
82	Mrs Theresa J C West	Courtesy C Bosanquet
84	Memorial to Cornwallis in All Saint's Church.	Paul French, Coolhat

Page	Caption	Credit
86	Images from The Admirals' Heritage Trail leaflet.	Shaun Stevens
87-97	Images on these pages are all from the unveiling ceremony and celebrations at Portsmouth on 16 June 2023.	Various
87	Left: Rev. Lynda Sebbage doing a reading at St Ann's Church. Portsmouth.	Peter Turner
87	Centre: The cross procession leaving St Ann's Church.	
87	Right: The Very Reverend Dr Anthony Cane, Dean of Portsmouth and Nigel Atkinson, HM Lord-Lieutenant of Hampshire.	
88	Images of The Very Reverend Dr Anthony Cane, Dean of Portsmouth and Nigel Atkinson, HM Lord-Lieutenant of Hampshire.	Paul French, Coolhat
89	Top: Images of The Very Reverend Dr Anthony Cane, Dean of Portsmouth and Nigel Atkinson, HM Lord-lieutenant of Hampshire after the unveiling.	
89	Bottom Left: Capt. Andrew Robinson RN, Captain of HMNB Portsmouth, The Very Reverend Dr Anthony Cane, Nigel Atkinson, HM Lord-Lieutenant of Hampshire and Councillor Tom Coles, Lord mayor of Portsmouth.	
89	Bottom Right: Mrs Karen Brett with Mr & Mrs Richard Cornwallis, all Cornwallis descendants.	
90	Top: Capt John Rodgaard (USN Ret), Capt Andrew Robinson RN, The Very Reverend Dr Anthony Cane, Nigel Atkinson, HM Lord-Lieutenant of Hampshire, Councillor Tom Coles and Chris Hobby.	
90	Bottom: Stephen Tregidgo, Barry Jolly, Capt Andrew Robinson RN, The Very Reverend Dr Anthony Cane, Capt John Rodgaard (USN Ret)(behind), Nigel Atkinson, HM Lord-Lieutenant of Hampshire, Councillor Tom Coles, Chris Hobby and John Bewley MBE.	
91	Top: Members of MoSHRS	
91	Bottom: Members of The 1805 Club	
92	Top: Cadet attendants at HMNB Portsmouth.	
92	Bottom: Members of MoSHRS choir	
93-96	Images from the Garden Party in the garden of Admiralty House, including Prof Andrew Lambert's presentation about Admiral Cornwallis.	
97	Images of mutual gift presentations between John Rodgaard of The 1805 Club and Chris Hobby of MoSHRS.	
98	Images from the celebrations 'On the Green' at Milford-on-Sea on 5-7 July 2019.	Bob Braid MoSHRS
99	Images of the memorial window being installed at All Saint's Church in 2019.	Bob Braid MoSHRS
100	Images of the 'Command of the Seas: The Navy and the New Forest Against Napoleon' Exhibition, St Barbe Museum and Art Gallery, Lymington; 8 June to 1 September 2019." organised jointly by MoSHRS, New Forest National Park Authority and St Barbe.	Paul French, Coolhat
101-103	Images of the formal dinner at the Cornwallis Suite of the South Lawns Hotel on 6 July 2019.	Bob Braid MoSHRS
104	Images from the visit to Buckler's Hard on 6 July 2019.	Bob Braid MoSHRS
105	All Saint's Church, Milford-on-Sea.	Paul French, Coolhat
107	*Admiral The Honourable Sir William Cornwallis GCB* after Daniel Gardner 1775.	National Maritime Museum
Endispiece	Newlands Manor.	Keith Evans, The 1805 Club
Back Cover	The Three Admirals Memorial Window.	Bob Braid MoSHRS

ARTICLES RELATING TO CORNWALLIS AND THE FRENCH REVOLUTIONARY & NAPOLEONIC WARS BY MEMBERS OF MILFORD-ON-SEA HISTORICAL RECORD SOCIETY WHICH HAVE INFORMED THE CORNWALLIS REMEMBERED PROJECT IN ALL ASPECTS OVER THE PAST SEVERAL YEARS

Barry Jolly: *Mrs. Whitby's Locket - The story of Captain John Whitby - probably England's youngest ever naval captain - and his redoubtable wife* Milford-on-Sea Historical Record Society 2011

Barry Jolly: 'A Good Man in Every Sense of the Word: The reputation of Admiral Robert Man' in *The Mariner's Mirror, The International Quarterly Journal of The Society for Nautical Research*, May 2018

Daphne Austin & Barry Jolly: "A Man's a Man for A' That: A clarification of the identity of each Robert Man' *Topmasts* No. 27, The Quarterly Newsletter of The Society for Nautical Research, August 2018

Barry Jolly: 'Poetry or autobiography? – The verses of a Victorian lady' *Milford-on-Sea Historical Record Society Occasional Magazine* NS 5 2018

Barry Jolly: 'The Three Admirals Window at Milford-on-Sea' *The Glazier* Summer 2019

Barry Jolly: 'A Resume of Local Naval and Military Personnel at the Time of the French Revolutionary and Napoleonic Wars' *Milford-on-Sea Historical Record Society Occasional Magazine* NS 6 2019

Chris Sanders 'The Church at Milford in the tides of war 1793-1815' *Milford-on-Sea Historical Record Society Occasional Magazine* NS 6 2019

Barry Jolly: 'The Bi-centenary of the Death of Admiral Cornwallis' *Hampshire Field Club and Archaeological Society Newsletter* Spring 2019

Chris Sanders: 'The funeral of Admiral Sir William Cornwallis' *Milford-on-Sea Historical Record Society Occasional Magazine* NS 6 2019

Barry Jolly: 'Rear-Admiral John Peyton: A Personal and Professional Re-Appraisal' *The Trafalgar Chronicle* NS4, 2019

Barry Jolly: 'Cornwallis and Hampshire' *Hampshire Studies: Proceedings of the Hampshire Field Club and Archaeological Society* Vol 74 2019

Bob Braid and Barry Jolly 'Introduction: Milford then and now' *Milford-on-Sea Historical Record Society Occasional Magazine* NS 6 2019

Ian Stevenson 'Nelson's friend in the Forest' *Milford-on-Sea Historical Record Society Occasional Magazine* NS 6 2019

Barry Jolly: 'Admiral Sir William Cornwallis - Aspects of a Life' *Milford-on-Sea Historical Record Society Occasional Magazine* NS 6 2019

Chris Hobby and Adam Smith 'The Milford and Milton Yeomanry' *Milford-on-Sea Historical Record Society Occasional Magazine* NS 6 2019

Barry Jolly: 'Elegy for the Admirals of Milford' *Milford-on-Sea Historical Record Society Occasional Magazine* NS 6 2019

Barry Jolly: 'Rear Admiral John Peyton: a member of Nelson's 'Band of Brothers'' *Milford-on-Sea Historical Record Society Occasional Magazine* NS 6 2019

Daphne Austin and Barry Jolly: 'Admiral Robert Man: Scion of A Naval Dynasty' *Milford-on-Sea Historical Record Society Occasional Magazine* NS 6 2019

Chris Sanders: 'Coda: The funeral of Admiral Sir William Cornwallis' *Milford-on-Sea Historical Record Society Occasional Magazine* NS 7 2021

Barry Jolly: 'Cornwallis, A Woman Named Cuba, and the Caribbean' *The Trafalgar Chronicle* NS5, 2020

Barry Jolly: 'Honouring Cornwallis' *The Kedge Anchor, The Magazine of The 1805 Club* April 2023

Together with the articles already submitted for this Cornwallis Memorial Decade book:

Barry Jolly: 'A Poetic Tribute' *See page 20*

Barry Jolly 'The pre-history of the collaboration between Milford-on-Sea Historical Record Society and the 1805 Club' *See page 43*

Barry Jolly: 'Command of the Seas – The Navy and the New Forest Against Napoleon' *See page 78*

Barry Jolly 'The Source of the Inscription on the Cornwallis Memorial Tablet' *See page 82*